TO:

....

FROM:

....

DATE:

....

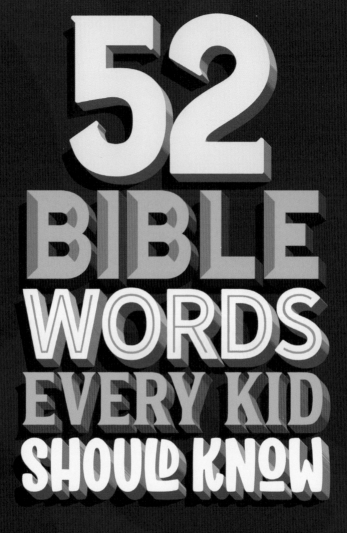

52 BIBLE WORDS EVERY KID SHOULD KNOW

CARRIE MARRS

ILLUSTRATED BY STEVEN WOOD

An Imprint of Thomas Nelson

52 Bible Words Every Kid Should Know

© 2021 Thomas Nelson

Tommy Nelson, PO Box 141000, Nashville, TN 37214

Published in Nashville, Tennessee, by Tommy Nelson. Tommy Nelson is an imprint of Thomas Nelson. Thomas Nelson is a registered trademark of HarperCollins Christian Publishing, Inc.

Tommy Nelson titles may be purchased in bulk for educational, business, fund-raising, or sales promotional use. For information, please e-mail SpecialMarkets@ThomasNelson.com.

Pronunciation keys are from *Merriam-Webster, Unabridged*, accessed June 12, 2020, https://unabridged.merriam-webster.com/.

Scripture quotations marked ICB are taken from the International Children's Bible®. Copyright © 1986, 1988, 1999, 2015 by Thomas Nelson. Used by permission. All rights reserved. Scripture quotations marked NIV are taken from the Holy Bible, New International Version®, NIV®. Copyright © 1973, 1978, 1984, 2011 by Biblica, Inc.® Used by permission of Zondervan. All rights reserved worldwide. www.Zondervan.com. The "NIV" and "New International Version" are trademarks registered in the United States Patent and Trademark Office by Biblica, Inc.® Scripture quotations marked NLT are taken from the Holy Bible, New Living Translation. © 1996, 2004, 2015 by Tyndale House Foundation. Used by permission of Tyndale House Publishers, a Division of Tyndale House Ministries, Carol Stream, Illinois 60188. All rights reserved.

ISBN 978-1-4002-1983-4 (eBook)

Library of Congress Cataloging-in-Publication Data

Names: Marrs, Carrie, author. | Wood, Steve (Illustrator), illustrator.
Title: 52 Bible words every kid should know / Carrie Marrs, illustrated by
  Steven Wood.
Other titles: Fifty-two Bible words every kid should know
Description: Nashville, Tennessee, USA : Thomas Nelson, 2021. | Audience:
  Ages 6-10 | Summary: "An engaging introduction to essential Bible terms,
  52 Bible Words Every Kid Should Know is a 52-week devotional that equips
  kids with the knowledge they need to understand God's Word and grow in
  their faith"-- Provided by publisher.
Identifiers: LCCN 2020025715 (print) | LCCN 2020025716 (ebook) | ISBN
  9781400219810 (hardcover) | ISBN 9781400219834 (epub)
Subjects: LCSH: Theology--Terminology--Juvenile literature. |
  Bible--Terminology--Juvenile literature. | Devotional
  literature--Juvenile literature.
Classification: LCC BR96.5 .M27 2021 (print) | LCC BR96.5 (ebook) | DDC
  242/.62--dc23
LC record available at https://lccn.loc.gov/2020025715
LC ebook record available at https://lccn.loc.gov/2020025716
ISBN 978-1-4002-1981-0
Written by Carrie Marrs; illustrated by Steven Wood

Printed in South Korea

21 22 23 24 25   Samhwa   10 9 8 7 6 5 4 3 2 1
Mfr: Samhwa / Seoul, South Korea / January 2021 / PO #9589871

All Scripture is inspired by God and is useful to teach us what is true and to make us realize what is wrong in our lives. It corrects us when we are wrong and teaches us to do what is right. God uses it to prepare and equip his people to do every good work.

—2 TIMOTHY 3:16-17 NLT

CONTENTS

LETTER TO PARENTS

Dear Parents,

Don't you love the moments when your children's eyes light up and they say, "Oh, I get it!"?

How amazing is it that we get to see their brains develop—neurons firing, ideas clicking and connecting, concepts settling into place? And as parents who love God, what's more meaningful than seeing our kids grasp more and more of His truth and power?

This book was made to help your kids do exactly that. It's a devotional that can even serve as an introductory overview of the Christian faith.

I'm not proud to admit that, although I grew up in the church, plenty of the topics in this book were blurry for me *for years*. After countless hours spent in Sunday school, words like *covenant*, *righteousness*, and *redemption* still zoomed right over my head. *Reconciliation? Sanctification?* I couldn't even pronounce those. Others I recognized—like *grace*, *worship*, *will*, and *glory*—but I wasn't sure where you could find them in the Bible or what they meant for my life.

In other words, I wish I'd had a resource like this when I was growing up. It would've provided so much clarity for me!

That wish took on new urgency as I looked at my own curious-but-squirrelly six-year-old. I wanted to create a book that would capture her attention and pique her interest—so she became a vital part of the writing process. I read entries out loud to her, and if she wasn't tracking, it was time to rewrite. If she was giggling or eagerly answering questions, I knew we were on the right track.

More than anything, I wanted to provide a resource that would lay the groundwork for my daughter to have a lifelong adventure of knowing and loving God. I pray this book will do the same thing for your dear young ones.

In each entry of this devotional, you'll see an important Bible word, a simple definition, and a discussion of that word using kid-friendly terms and kid-level examples. Then you'll see where this concept can be found in the Bible and a related hands-on activity.

This book will help your children learn facts—like how many books are in the Bible or who wrote almost half of Psalms—but it will do much more. It will help them begin to see how these theological truths fit into God's big story of redemption and His relationship with us. Learning these important words from Scripture will become an entryway to an expanded view of how big God's heart is for His people.

May this book open your children's minds to the wonders of His story and open their hearts to the enormity of His love. May it pull them into Scripture and help them feel closer to the One who is constantly reaching out to them and pouring out love to them every day.

Carrie Marrs

1

CREATION

noun   \krē-'ā-shən\

~~~~

God's act of making something new

When you bring home something you made at school, like a painting, you feel proud as you hand it to your mom. It's special because *you* made it. It even shows something about you—what colors you like, how good you are at painting, or what you can imagine. Your mom might say, "Wow, this is some great work you did! I like how you gave the elephants purple polka dots" or "I like the sun with the smiley face."

When we look at people and the world around us—sand and mountains, animals and plants, sunlight and rain—we see what God created. And we can see what God is like when we look at what He made. We feel His power in thunder and big ocean waves, and we see His beauty in bright flowers and pretty sunsets. We can

FiND It
IN THE BIBLE

GENESIS 1

The story of the world began when God decided to make it. All He had to do was say, "Let there be light," and there was light. And He created everything out of nothing! He made the land and seas, the sun and moon, and the plants and animals, and He called them good. Then He made people and called them *very* good. God created everything over six days. On the seventh day, He rested.

tell He's good when He gives us tasty food from the earth. We feel His love and joy when we hug our dad or giggle with a friend.

Signs of God's knowledge, love, and life are everywhere, and they all give us reasons to worship and trust Him. They also give us reasons to be happy!

See how many things you can notice today that show God's creative power. Then tell God what you love about what He's made.

~~~~~~~~~~~~

God, I praise You for creating this whole world. You are amazing! Today, my favorite thing You made is _____ .

TRY it OUT

Create something of your own using whatever supplies you can find—paper, glue, scissors, markers, a paper towel roll, or yarn. Make the shape of a person or animal. This is your creation! Now step away from all the supplies and make something else out of nothing. Wait, you can't do that, can you? Only God can create something from nothing!

2

BIBLE

noun \\'bī-bəl\\

God's story and His message for us in writing

ou lead the way!" your dad says as you walk into the zoo.

"Okay!" you reply, although you've never been there before. What will you need to help you? A map? Maybe some signs with arrows? It'd be a lot harder to find your way without those to guide you!

The Bible is like a map or arrow—it's our guide for life. It is God's Word, or His message, to us. The Bible tells us the truth about who God is, why we should love and obey Him, and how we can do that.

God's Word has sixty-six books, or parts, full of stories, rules, poems, and letters. Can you guess how many people wrote it? It was more than one or two. It was about forty people! And it was

FiND It

IN THE BIBLE

LUKE 4:17–21

One day Jesus was in the temple, a place where people worshiped God. He stood up and read God's Word out loud. He picked a part that had been written by Isaiah, one of God's messengers. It was about how God would someday send a savior—it was talking about Jesus! He read the words, "God sent me to tell the prisoners of sin that they are free." Then Jesus said, "While you heard these words just now, they were coming true!" (vv. 18, 21 ICB).

written over a really long time—about *fifteen hundred* years. God spoke to these people about what to write, so that's why it's called God's Word.

The Bible tells us about special messengers who said God would send someone to save people from their sins and how Jesus came and did just that. We learn what Jesus taught and how He lived. We hear how His followers learned to love God and other people, how they worshiped God, and that someday God's family will live with Him in heaven.

All of this comes together to make one big story about God.

~~~~~~~~~~~~

God, thank You for giving me important messages through the Bible. Help me know Your story even better.

TRY it OUT

God gives us important messages through the Bible, but we need to spend time with the Bible to understand them. The same is true when you decode a message. Crack this code by replacing each letter with the letter that comes before it in the alphabet (for example, *B* becomes *A*):

Hpe tqfblt up vt uispvhi uif Cjcmf.

3

PRAYER

noun \\'prer\\

a talk
with God

H as someone ever asked you to pray, and you didn't know what to say? Everyone has felt that way. We don't want to do it wrong, and we're not sure how to do it right.

God doesn't want us to be so worried about praying the right way that we don't pray at all. He wants to hear from us because He loves us.

When a friend says hello to you, they're showing that they like you and want to talk with you. God has a way of doing that too.

God actually started a conversation with us by showing Himself through creation and speaking to us through the Bible. Prayer is our turn to talk back. He's inviting us to come closer to Him and to know Him and His love.

So what do we say to God? Anything that is honest. We don't have to use fancy words. We can say, "Wow! The sky is so beautiful!" Or we can tell Him, "Thank You for macaroni and cheese

FiND It

IN THE BIBLE

ACTS 12

Sometimes God answers our prayers in *big* ways. Take, for example, the apostle Peter. He was put in prison because he'd been teaching people about Jesus. There were chains holding him down and sixteen soldiers guarding the jail, but his Christian friends kept praying that God would save Peter. One night an angel suddenly appeared, and Peter's chains fell off! The angel led him safely out of jail. God had answered His people's prayers with an incredible rescue.

and for my best friend." We can tell Him anything, including the wrong things we've done, and ask for forgiveness. We might also say, "Help me be loving and not selfish today."

Whenever we need help, we can go to God. He's a good, powerful Father! We might see Him make a sick person healthy again or bring us a friend when we're lonely.

Does God only hear us when our eyes are closed or when we're at church? Nope! We can talk to God anytime and anywhere. He always hears us!

~~~~~~~~~~~

God, thank You for wanting to be close
to me and for listening to me.

TRY it OUT

Ask a family member you don't see often to try something with you. Talk to each other on the phone every day for a week. Afterward, ask yourself, *Do I feel closer to this person?* You probably will! The more we talk and listen to someone—whether it's a family member, a friend, or God—the closer relationship we'll have with them.

4

HEAVEN

noun   \'he-vən\

God's home and kingdom

When God made the world, it was perfect. But when sin came into the world, it brought pain, sadness, and death. Our sin separated us from God. So God said, "I will make a way for them to come back home to Me." He promised to prepare a place for us, a perfect place called heaven.

In heaven, God is the King. Everyone in His kingdom becomes part of His royal family. It's like God has a giant castle where people become His princes and princesses. When we put our faith in Jesus, we become part of God's kingdom. Heaven becomes our new home—it's where we really belong. We know we'll be there someday, after our time on earth, and we get so excited just thinking about it!

God loves to give amazing gifts to His children, and He's

FiND It

IN THE BIBLE

REVELATION 1, 5, 21–22

Jesus gave one of His followers, John, a vision of heaven. It gives us an idea of how awesome heaven will be. In the vision, thousands of angels sing praises to Jesus, who's on a throne. A crystal-clear river called the *water of life* flows from His throne. There's a golden city, glittering like jewels, and there's no sun because God Himself shines so brightly. There's no more night or darkness. People see God's face, and He wipes away their tears. God sits on the throne and says, "Look! I am making everything new!" (Revelation 21:5 ICB).

preparing a lot of wonderful surprises for us in heaven. There are a few things, though, that He said we can count on.

First of all, we'll never get hurt or feel bad. Remember the last time you tripped and scraped your knee? That won't happen in heaven. Do you and your brother or sister usually fight about what show to watch? That won't happen either! In heaven, we'll never be sad about missing someone or feel scared in the dark. Everyone in God's family, from all throughout history, will be there together. And we'll all be happier than we've ever been. Can you guess why? Because we'll be close with God and thrilled to be living in His awesome kingdom.

Heaven will be a perfect, beautiful place where we'll live forever with our good Father and King. Whatever we can imagine, heaven will be even better!

God, I can't wait to go to my true home and live with You forever!

TRY it OUT

Draw a picture of what you think heaven could be like.

ETERNAL

adjective   \ē'tərnᵊl\

having no
beginning
or end

Have you noticed that some things don't last very long? Flowers bloom only a few days. Bread turns dry and stale. Toys break after you play with them a lot.

Did you know this world won't last forever?

The world had a beginning, and it will have an end. But God is eternal, which means He has no beginning or end. It's like the entire universe is inside a snow globe and God is outside it. Time ticks away only inside the snow globe, and God watches from above.

We're not eternal either. How can we know that? Because we have birthdays! Our birthdays celebrate when we were born because we weren't alive before that. And though our bodies won't last forever, our souls will.

God says that while we're in this world, we should care most about what will last forever. Do you know what lasts forever? Our

FiND It

IN THE BIBLE

PSALM 9; PSALM 145

David loved God more than anything. When David was in trouble, He went to God for help. When he sinned, he asked for forgiveness. He cared about what God cared about. Why? Because David knew God is eternal and that what He says is most important. David said, "The Lord rules forever. He sits on his throne to judge. The Lord will judge the world by what is right." (Psalm 9:7–8 ICB). David was a king, but he knew that God is the eternal King. He said to God, "Your kingdom will continue forever" (Psalm 145:13 ICB).

relationship with God and loving and helping others. If we act like those things are super important, they'll become our *treasure*—and it's the only kind of treasure that lasts forever.

Sometimes all we can think about is getting a fun toy or winning a game. But if that's all we ever do, we'll get to heaven and see those things didn't matter as much we thought. They came to an end, just like the world did! Instead, we want to go to heaven and say, "Hey, here's everything I cared about when I was on earth. It's so important that it lasts forever!"

God, help me care about what lasts forever
so my treasures will be in heaven.

TRY it OUT

Put some sugar and sand in a jar. Add water and stir it. What happens? The sand stays while the sugar dissolves—you can't see the sugar anymore. It's like it goes away. God is like the sand, which you can still see. God has no end, but the earth *will* come to an end.

TRINITY

noun \ˈtrinətē\

~~~

God the Father, God the Son, and God the Holy Spirit

Have you ever heard someone explain something, but you didn't understand it?

There are some things about God we can't fully understand—and that's okay. That means He's bigger than what our minds can hold. But we keep trying to understand Him because we love Him.

One crazy, mysterious thing about God is called the *Trinity*, which means "three in one." There's only one God, yet there are three Persons who are God. There's God the Father, God the Son, and God the Holy Spirit. They're each distinct, or separate, from each other—that means the Father isn't the Son, the Son isn't the Spirit, and the Spirit isn't the Father. But each of them is the one God of the Bible.

If you're thinking, *Whoa, what?* then you're like everyone else! Just keep listening to what the Bible says.

In the beginning of the world, God said, "Let us make human

FiND It

IN THE BIBLE

MATTHEW 3:13–17

The word *Trinity* isn't in the Bible, but all three Persons are in it. Just take a look at Jesus' baptism. When Jesus came up out of the water, heaven opened. The Holy Spirit came down on Him like a dove. God's voice came down from heaven and said, "This is my Son and I love him. I am very pleased with him" (v. 17 ICB).

beings in our image and likeness" (Genesis 1:26 ICB). The Father, Jesus, and the Holy Spirit created everything together.

Jesus taught people to pray to the Father in His own name. He sent the Holy Spirit to guide people and change their hearts. He told His disciples to baptize people in the name of the Father, the Son, and the Holy Spirit.

All three are their own person. All three are the one God.

God blows our minds, right? And why shouldn't He? He is God, and we're not. There's no one like Him!

~~~~~~~~~~~~~~~

God, You are wild and amazing, and I worship You because You are bigger than I can understand!

TRY it OUT

The Trinity is a mystery we'll never really understand. It's too big and wonderful for our minds! But some people have noticed that God left clues about the Trinity in the beautiful world He created. For example, a three-leaf clover has three leaves, but it is one plant. An egg has a shell, a yolk, and a white part, yet it's one piece of food. These things aren't exactly like the Trinity, but they help us think about it and open our hearts to this mystery. Can you think of any other clues in creation that show this "three-in-one" idea?

SOVEREIGNTY

noun   \ˈsä-v(ə-)rən-tē\

- God's power
and right
to rule
everything

Who's in charge of a classroom? A teacher. Who's in charge of a school? A principal. Who's in charge of a town? A mayor. And who's in charge of a country? A president or king.

Each of those people is in charge of a certain area. God is in charge too—but in charge of what?

Everything! He's the one who created all things, so He's the one in charge of it all. First Chronicles 29:11 says, "Everything in heaven and on earth belongs to you. . . . You are the ruler over everything" (ICB).

God is a king who sits on a throne in heaven, where everyone bows to worship Him. He is the King of kings and Lord of lords—more powerful than anyone else in charge. In fact, they're in charge only because He has said, "I'll let you be in charge."

FiND It

IN THE BIBLE

JONAH 1–4

If Jonah ever questioned if God was in control, he didn't have to wonder after his journey! God told Jonah to go to Nineveh and tell the people how to follow Him. But Jonah didn't want to, so he hopped on a boat going away from Nineveh. Then God brought a big storm, and Jonah was tossed into the sea. God caused a fish to swallow Jonah and then, after a while, spit him back out. God definitely got Jonah's attention by showing His power! In the end Jonah obeyed, doing his part in God's plan to help the people of Nineveh.

Nothing can happen unless God allows it, and nothing can get in the way of His plans.

God rules over plants, animals, weather, and people. He puts us in situations where we can be challenged and grow. And even though He doesn't want bad things to happen, when they do, God makes sure something good comes out of it.

Picture it like this: a man is making a clay pot. He holds the clay in his hands and shapes it into whatever type of pot he wants. Jeremiah 18:1–6 says that's how God is with us. We are in His hands!

———

God, I praise You for being the King in charge of everything.
Thank You for watching over me. I know I'm in Your hands.

TRY it OUT

Grab some Play-Doh, and make whatever shapes you want with it. You're in charge of what each shape becomes. As you hold it in your hands, try to imagine God doing the same thing with you and everything around you.

8

RIGHTEOUSNESS

noun \rī-chəs-ness\

**being perfect
and always right**

T hink of a time you gave the right answer to a question in school. Did you feel excited? It feels nice to have the right answer because we can't be right all the time.

But there *is* someone who's right all the time. You probably can guess who. God! The Bible says He is righteous—everything He does is right. He's perfect, pure, and good. He'll never do something wrong because that would go against who He is.

Think about it like this: Can a hippo fly in the sky? Can a slug outrun a cheetah? No! It's not in their nature to do those things. That's not how they were made. In the same way, it's not in God's nature to be wrong.

FiND It

IN THE BIBLE

---

1 SAMUEL 24

When we do the right thing, it's like we're showing other people God's righteousness. Take a look at 1 Samuel 24. King Saul was mad at David because God had chosen David to become the new king. King Saul tried to hurt David, so David ran away. While David was hiding in a cave, Saul walked into it, not knowing David was there. It was the perfect chance for David to sneak up on Saul and hurt him, but David chose not to. When Saul found out, he was shocked. He said to David, "You are more righteous than I am. You treated me well even after I treated you badly. May God reward you for doing what was right!"

Psalm 119 says, "Lord, you do what is right. . . . The rules you commanded are right" (vv. 137–138 ICB). God is always the one who can decide what's right. We can't do that on our own. So God gave us rules to help us and guide us in the right way to live.

Every time we read a command in the Bible, it's like God is sharing a secret with us. "This is what really matters," He whispers. "Trust My wisdom."

We'll never be perfect on earth, but God wants us to keep trying to learn and do what is right. He will help us do the right thing too. Just ask!

~~~~~~~~~~~~~~~~

God, I praise You for always being right!

TRY it OUT

Take out your favorite puzzle and start working on it. When you find a puzzle piece that fits, think, *That's the right piece. That's the only one that's right.* God and His good rules are the same way. Only God is right. Only what He says to do is right.

9

JUSTICE

noun   \'jə-stəs\

what is
right and fair
for everyone

I magine that one day at lunchtime a bigger classmate takes a smaller classmate's food. The smaller classmate looks like she might cry while the bigger classmate laughs.

Do you think that would be okay? Not at all!

Do you think God would say that would be okay? No way. He'd say that's not only mean but unfair. God can always tell us what is fair because He is *just*. And just as a compass points north, justice always points to what's right.

Psalm 146 says, "The Lord does what is fair for those who have been wronged. He gives food to the hungry . . . [and] lifts up people who are in trouble. . . . But he overthrows the wicked" (vv. 7–9 ICB). God is like the best superhero ever! He sets things right. He helps weak people and stops the bad guys.

God wants us to be just like Him. If we see something unfair happening, we should step in and help make things fair. We can become superheroes too!

FiND It

IN THE BIBLE

LUKE 18:1–8

Jesus told a story about a judge who wasn't just. The judge didn't care about the people in his town. One woman kept coming to him, saying, "There's a man who's not being fair to me. Help me. Make this right!" The judge didn't want to help, but he eventually agreed to help because the woman wouldn't stop asking. Jesus said, "God is far better than this bad judge. So don't stop asking Him to make things right. God will help His people!"

God is also the judge of the world. Whenever anyone does something wrong, God's justice requires that there be a consequence for it.

What is a consequence? Let's say a teacher finds out about that big classmate who took the little classmate's food, and she sends him to the principal. That would be a consequence of the wrong choice he made.

When we sin, there are consequences too. Because God is just, He won't pretend we don't do wrong things. That would be like if your parents just covered their eyes while your brother or sister kept stomping on your favorite toy! Instead, God sent Jesus to die on the cross so that Jesus could take on all the consequences of our sins for us.

~~~~~~~~~~~~~~

God, thank You for Your justice. Help me
be like You and do what is fair.

TRY it OUT

Get out some treats, and give one to each family member. Then have your brother or sister play along by snatching a treat from someone else. Say to the thief, "That's not fair. Please give it back." This will be practice for helping to make the world just!

10

HOLY

adjective \ˈhō-lē\

pure and
set apart

Would you ever use your toothbrush to scrub the floor and then put it in your mouth? Ew, no! You always make sure your toothbrush is clean, right? That way it's set apart for a special activity.

God wants His people to be set apart for a special activity too—for worshiping Him. And just like we need to use a clean toothbrush to brush our teeth, we need to be clean from sin to worship God.

You see, God is holy, which means He's pure and there's no sin in Him. But people are sinful, which means they don't always do what's right. God wanted a special group of people, the Israelites, to be set apart from everyone else. He said, "You must be holy because I am holy" (Leviticus 19:2 ICB).

God gave the Israelites rules that helped them to do good and love one another.

FiND It

IN THE BIBLE

EXODUS 3:1–6

One day Moses was taking care of some sheep when he saw a burning bush. He walked up to it to see what was going on. God called Moses' name from the bush and said, "Don't come closer. Take off your sandals. You're standing on holy ground." Moses obeyed because he knew how pure, important, and powerful God is. He covered his face to show respect. Moses knew that any place where God is becomes a special and holy place.

It's like if you went to a friend's house covered in mud. You left dark footprints in every room, and at snack time, glops of mud fell from your sleeve into your friend's bowl! Afterward, your mom made a rule: always take a shower before playdates.

When the Israelites did what God said, they'd be holy. They could worship Him and show the world how good He is.

Nowadays anyone who follows Jesus can be one of God's holy people too. Colossians 3 says, "God has chosen you and made you his holy people. He loves you. So always . . . be kind, humble, gentle, and patient. . . . Forgive each other. . . . Love each other" (vv. 12–14 ICB). When we do those things, we worship God and show the world how good He is!

~~~~~~~~~~~

God, I want to be holy like You. Help me
do what is pure, good, and loving.

TRY it OUT

The next time you put on pajamas, think about how they are clothes set apart for bedtime. This is just like how we're set apart for obeying God so that we can be pure and loving like Him.

WORSHIP

verb   \ˈwȯr-shəp\

~~~

**giving praise
and showing
honor**

What's something you own that's important to you? Think about how you treat it. Do you bury it under clothes and ignore it? Do you step on it? No! You are careful with it and put it in a special place, like on the shelf in your room. When anyone walks in, they'll see how special it is.

God can see how important He is to us by the way we treat Him. If He has a special place in our lives, then we can show Him how much we love Him by worshiping Him. When we worship, we're saying, "You're the most amazing and most important!"

How do we worship?

By singing songs to God and praying, by reading the Bible and obeying, and by loving and helping others. Worship is anything we do to show God that He deserves our time, attention, and hard work.

Why should we worship God?

FiND It

IN THE BIBLE

DANIEL 6

Daniel worshiped God every day. He prayed, memorized God's Word, and obeyed God. When he moved to a country where almost no one else worshiped God, Daniel thought, *I won't quit. I'll still worship God.* When a new law said he wasn't allowed to pray to God, Daniel thought, *That won't stop me!* Daniel was put in a lions' den as punishment for praying to God, but God kept him safe. The king of the land said, "Everyone must now respect Daniel's God—the one true God!"

Because He's wonderful! He's perfect and powerful. He made us and takes care of us. We don't worship Him to get a reward. We do it out of love for Him. It's just like why you give someone a hug—you do it because you love them.

Worship is what happens at church on Sunday, but it's also anything you do during the week to honor God, like saying a prayer or sharing with a friend. Our worship not only honors God—it also shows others how awesome He is! It's like we're putting a giant spotlight on Him and His greatness.

~~~~~~~~~~~~~~~~~

God, I want to worship You every day. I think You're amazing!

TRY it OUT

Look at the worship activities below. Try to do one activity a day for a week. It's not about being perfect. It's about showing God you love Him by trying.

1. Singing a song about how good God is
2. Praying
3. Reading the Bible
4. Obeying
5. Showing love to someone
6. Helping someone
7. Giving to someone in need

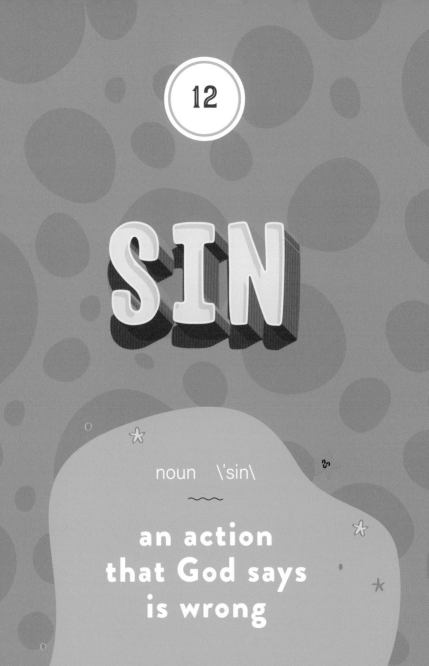

12

SIN

noun   \'sin\

an action
that God says
is wrong

Crash! A ball you threw hits your mom's flower vase. When she walks in the room, you point to your brother and say, "He broke it!"

Even if you don't get in trouble with Mom, you've lied, which God says is a sin.

The Bible teaches us what is right and wrong by giving us commands: Do not lie, steal, or hurt people. Love God and love others. Keep your promises. A sin is anything we do that is not pure or good or that goes against what God says is best for us.

Sin hurts the people around us, and it hurts our own hearts. But most of all, it becomes a big problem in our relationship with God. It's like if you had a friend who kept stealing your things. That would become a problem in your relationship, wouldn't it?

God is holy and pure, so sin separates us from Him. He is also just—He keeps things right and fair—and His justice says there

FiND It

IN THE BIBLE

GENESIS 3

Do you remember where the first sin happened in the Bible? It was in the garden of Eden. God told Adam and Eve not to eat fruit from *one* tree. Later the fruit from that tree seemed so delicious that they went ahead and bit into it anyway. Their sin made God so sad. It meant that they had to move away from the garden—and farther away from Him.

has to be a consequence for sin. What is that consequence? Well, the Bible says, "The payment for sin is death" (Romans 6:23 ICB). Everyone has sinned, so the whole world is in this bad situation.

But guess what! God loves us so much. His love for us is as big as the universe. He doesn't want us to be separated from Him, even though we've sinned. That's why God sent Jesus to earth. He wanted to save us! Jesus made a way for us to be forgiven—not punished—and to become close with God again.

~~~~~~~~~~

God, thank You for showing us what is right and wrong.
I believe that what You say is right is right for me.

TRY it OUT

Pour some water in a clear cup. Add color to it—either by stirring a marker in it or by adding a drop of food coloring. Now add some oil (any kind) to the cup and stir it. Can you see how the oil and water stay separate? That's like how God and sin are—God is always separate from sin.

13

RECONCILIATION

noun \ˌre-kən-ˌsi-lē-ˈā-shən\

~~~~~~~~

the act of bringing together two people whose friendship is broken

I'm sorry," your friend says. After hurting each other's feelings, you two had stopped playing together. "I'm sorry too," you say as you give each other a high five. Now you're ready to play tag and ride your bikes together again.

Reconciliation means coming back together after fighting. When you and your friend were fighting, you couldn't talk and laugh together like normal. Your friendship had a problem. But after you apologized, you "fixed" your broken relationship. You were *reconciled*, which means you were friends again.

God created people to be close to Him. He wants us to feel His happiness and love, like He's giving us hugs and making us laugh. But God hates sin, so when we sinned, we became God's enemies. Sin broke our relationship with Him.

Sin also messed up the whole world. It brought in all the sad and painful parts of life, like fighting with friends or getting sick with a fever.

FiND It

IN THE BIBLE

GENESIS 25, 27, 33

Jacob and Esau were twin brothers who didn't get along. As the firstborn son, Esau was supposed to get their family's land and special blessings, but Jacob stole them. Esau was so angry that he wanted to hurt Jacob, so Jacob ran away. Years later, Jacob returned and bowed down before Esau as a way to say, "I'm sorry. Will you forgive me?" Esau hugged and kissed Jacob as a way to say, "I forgive you!" These two brothers fixed their relationship. They were reconciled!

This all made God very sad, so He made a way to fix everything sin messed up. And He did it through Jesus.

Colossians 1 says, "God decided to bring all things back to himself again. . . . At one time you were separated from God. You were God's enemies . . . because the evil deeds you did were against God. But now Christ has made you God's friends again" (vv. 20–22 ICB).

Even though we're the ones who had messed up and hurt Him, God made a way to fix our friendship. That's how amazing He is!

~~~~~~~~~~~~~~~~~

God, thank You for sending Jesus so
that we can be friends again!

TRY it OUT

Get three Legos and connect two of them by placing the other Lego on top of them. Imagine those two Legos on the bottom are like you and God. Now imagine that you sin so you are now separated from God. Remove the Lego on top so that the two bottom pieces (you and God) are separated. Put that top Lego back on them, and this time think of it like Jesus bringing you back to God.

14

COVENANT

noun   \'kəv-nənt\

an agreement
of promises

Imagine your dad says, "We need to work on keeping your room cleaner. Let's make a deal. Every Saturday, if it's clean, I'll take you to the donut shop." You shake hands and both say, "I promise!"

God made promises with people called *covenants*. He promised to give them good things and have a close friendship with them. In return, they promised to obey and love God.

In His covenant with Abraham, God promised to bless him and everyone in the world through him.

In His covenant with the Israelites, He gave them rules for living. If they lived God's way, they'd show His goodness to the world.

In His covenant with David, God said someone in David's family would bring God's kingdom of peace to the world.

Do you think God did what He promised? Yes, always! Do you think the people did? Nope, they didn't. Imagine if you didn't do

FiND It

IN THE BIBLE

GENESIS 15, 17

One of the first covenants God made was with Abraham. God promised to give Abraham a big family, even though Abraham and his wife, Sarah, were old and had no children. Abraham must have thought, *How can that happen?* But he kept listening. God said, "Can you count all the stars in the sky? No! Your family will get really big, and like the stars, there will be too many to count." Sure enough, later Sarah had a baby, who was the start of a big, new family.

your part in the deal with your dad, and your room was always a mess of stinky clothes and toys. "Pee-yoo!" your dad would say every Saturday. "No donut shop today."

God saw that His people needed help, so He made a new covenant. This time Jesus would come and do what everyone before Him couldn't. He obeyed God perfectly!

Can *we* do what Jesus did? No, we mess up all the time. But if our faith is in Jesus, we can receive good things from God and have a close friendship with Him.

God does something else amazing through the new covenant: He changes our hearts. He helps us love what He loves and *want* to do what He says is good!

God, thank You for always keeping Your promises.

TRY it OUT

Get on a teeter-totter with a friend. Notice how you both have to do your part for it to work? It's the same way with covenants. Both God and the people promised to do their parts for God to bless the people.

15

LAW

noun \'lȯ\
~~~~~~~~~~

the rules God gave
Israel to make the
Israelites righteous
and loving

Have you ever heard of the Golden Rule? It came from something Jesus said: "Do for other people the same things you want them to do for you" (Matthew 7:12 ICB). It's called *golden* because it's such a good rule. It helps people know how to be kind.

God gave the Israelites good rules called the *law*. All the rules showed how wise and righteous God is. They also showed people the best way to live to have a good and peaceful life.

God's people struggled to follow the law. The most famous rules of the law were the Ten Commandments. But there weren't just ten rules—there were more than six hundred! We read about them in the first five books of the Bible, along with a bunch of stories about the Israelites not following the rules. It's like if you were

FiND It

IN THE BIBLE

EXODUS 19–20, 24

Have you ever wondered what God's handwriting looks like? God wrote part of the law—the Ten Commandments—on stone tablets! Not long after Moses led the Israelites out of Egypt, Moses walked up a mountain, lightning flashed, and the ground shook. There God gave the Ten Commandments: "Worship God and no one else. Show Him respect. Have a day of rest. Obey your parents. Keep your promises. Don't be jealous or hurt anyone. Don't lie or steal." Then God gave Moses two stone tablets with the commands written on them to share with the Israelites. God's handwriting was probably really neat, but Moses would know for sure!

playing baseball and you missed the ball when you swung, over and over again. You kept striking out! The Israelites kept failing to trust and obey God.

When Jesus came to earth, He "fulfilled" the law, which means He followed God's commands when no one else could. Jesus also said the whole point of the law is really about two important commands: to love God and to love people. When we love like Jesus did, we fulfill the law too.

God, thank You for helping me to live Your way.

TRY it OUT

The next time you're in a car, ask the driver to name some driving rules. Then watch and try to spot each rule the driver is following. Is he stopping at stop signs? Waiting on another car before he turns? What would happen if he forgot those rules? Yikes! Someone could get hurt. He's following good rules that protect and take care of people. God's rules are like that too.

16

IDOL

noun   \\'ī-dəl\\

anything or
anyone we
treat as more
important
than God

Soccer is my favorite! It's all I ever want to do."

"Sophie is my best friend. I pretty much do whatever she does."

Maybe you've said something like that before. It's great to have favorite activities and best friends! But the Bible says we have to be careful to never love anything or anyone more than we love God. If we do, we're actually worshiping something other than Him.

When God was first teaching the Israelites how to live, they were surrounded by people who worshiped idols—fake gods. Sometimes the idols were gold statues. God said, "Never worship fake gods." Why? "Because," He said, "I am the one true God."

God is more powerful than anyone else. He is the One who created everything. He loves people, listens to them, and takes care of them. Could an idol do any of that? No way!

FiND It

IN THE BIBLE

1 KINGS 18

Once, when the Israelites were worshiping idols, Elijah said to the king, "Let's have a contest—your idol against my God." The king agreed. On a mountaintop, Elijah and the king's men built altars, or special places to offer gifts to their gods. Then they took turns praying for their gods to send fire. When the king's men went first, nothing happened. When Elijah prayed, God threw down so much fire from heaven that it burned up Elijah's altar and everything around it! Everybody could see that God is the one true God.

Idols look different these days. They're things we spend a lot of time thinking about or doing. They could be the stuff we have (like toys), activities (like games, TV, sports, or music), or people (like friends or famous people). If we ever act like something is more important than God, we're treating it like an idol. For example, maybe we want to skip church to play soccer, or maybe we make fun of someone just because our friends are doing it.

If we say God is the most important, then we won't let anything stop us from showing Him love. After all, nobody else is God. He is the one true God!

God, I want to worship only You, the one true God.

TRY it OUT

Pour some juice in a glass. Then pour some water in a second glass and add some food coloring so it looks like the juice. Have someone blindfold you. Then take a sip from each glass. Even though they look similar, you can taste the difference right away! That colored water is "fake juice," just like idols are fake gods.

SABBATH

noun \\'sabəth\\

God's special
day of rest

If you spent a week at camp playing wildly in the sun, how would you feel by Friday evening when the stars came out? Pretty tired, huh? You'd be ready for a good night's sleep and maybe a nap on Saturday.

God set up a special rest day for the Israelites called the *Sabbath*—but it wasn't because they had a crazy week at camp.

God created the Sabbath because He had taken a rest day after He created the world. And He wanted the Israelites to do something like that. So they'd work for six days and then take a break on the seventh day, just like He did. It's kind of like how you take a break for recess during the school day.

FiND It

IN THE BIBLE

EXODUS 16

Imagine that your stomach starts to grumble and you see something falling outside your window. Is it rain? No—it's hamburgers! Too crazy to believe? Well, something like that happened to the Israelites. When the Israelites were in the desert, God provided them with manna—bread that fell like rain from the sky. The people would gather it in baskets and then bake or boil it. It stayed good for only one day, except for the sixth day of every week. God sent extra that day and none at all the seventh day. That way the people could prepare enough food for two days and rest on the seventh day. They could just sit back, relax, spend time with God, and eat their delicious manna!

The Sabbath also reminded the Israelites that someday God would give them a resting place, a place called the *promised land*. Did you know we have a promised land too? We're not there yet, but someday we'll be in heaven with God. So for us, the Sabbath is a special time to look forward to heaven!

Christians today set aside a day each week to worship God at church and to be with people we love. This special day brings us closer to Him and makes us strong for whatever the following week brings.

~~~~~~~~~~

God, thank You for giving me rest.

TRY it OUT

Collect fourteen rocks, and paint two of them a bright color. Make a line of rocks with six unpainted rocks in a row and a colored rock at the end. Then make another row just like it underneath. The pattern is clear, isn't it? The colored rocks are like Sabbath days, which create a pattern for our lives week after week.

18

SACRIFICE

noun   \ˈsa-krə-ˌfīs\

**something
given up and
offered as a gift**

Have you ever given up something important to you just to make someone smile? Maybe there was a time when you gave your brother or sister the biggest piece of cake, even though you really wanted it.

That would be a *sacrifice*. The Israelites offered sacrifices to God to show their love for Him and to become closer to Him. They gave up some of their nicest things—their best bread and animals—as gifts for God. He had, after all, provided everything they had. This was a way to say, "Thank You, God!"

The Israelites set up an altar fire, which was kind of like a cooking grill. They'd put their gifts on the altar fire, and those gifts would become a smoke that floated up to the sky. God would receive them like sweet-smelling presents. Just think how happy someone is when you give them a present. The Israelites' presents for God made Him happy too!

FiND It

IN THE BIBLE

LEVITICUS 9

The first time the Israelites made sacrifices, everyone brought animals and grains to Aaron. He was a priest, which meant he was the leader for sacrifices. When he put the people's offerings in the altar fire, something surprising happened. God sent fire from the sky and completely burned up all the offerings on the altar. This showed that He accepted their gifts! The people shouted with joy and bowed down in worship.

There were also special sacrifices to deal with sin. The punishment for sin was death, but God didn't want that for His people. So He let the blood of an animal "cover over" the sin. The animal died in the place of the people who sinned.

These sacrifices didn't completely solve the problem of sin. They were a little bit like Band-Aids—they covered over sins but didn't take them away. They fixed the sin problem for the moment, but a better sacrifice would come later that would fix it forever—when Jesus died for our sins. What He did on the cross really does take away our sins.

*God, I want to make sacrifices
to show You my love.*

TRY it OUT

We don't need to offer the same kind of sacrifices the Israelites did, but we still want to give God gifts. If you have any money, you could put it in the offering plate at church. Or you could give a favorite toy to someone who doesn't have many. God says that giving gifts to people who need them is just like giving gifts to Him.

19

TABERNACLE

noun   \ˈtabə(r)ˌnakəl\
~~~

a beautiful
tent for God
to live in

ave you ever gone camping before? Who were you with? Maybe you got to play in the woods and make s'mores. At night you could use your flashlight in the dark and snuggle up in your sleeping bag. Best of all, you didn't even have to say good-bye to the people camping with you! It was an "outside sleepover," so you got to stay together.

Well, God did something like that with the Israelites. He made it so they'd never have to say good-bye to Him, even when they were living in tents in the wilderness and traveling a lot. God said, "Build a special tent just for Me, and I'll stay with you—wherever you go." This new tent would be called the *tabernacle*.

The Israelites couldn't run to the store to pick up supplies to build the tabernacle. So instead, they looked through their own belongings to see what they could give. They even gave up their

FiND It

IN THE BIBLE

EXODUS 35:31–35; 36:1; 39:32

Bezalel and Oholiab were great at making things and could handle any tricky task. When it was time to build the tabernacle, they said, "We're ready to work!" Other people said, "We want to help, but we don't know how to carve wood, sew, or cut designs in stone." Bezalel and Oholiab said, "No problem! We'll show you how." Everyone worked hard for months. When the tabernacle was finally done, they were so proud of what they had built together.

fanciest stuff—shiny gold objects, pretty cloths, and sparkly jewels! They wanted to help make the tabernacle really beautiful.

Once the tabernacle was built, only the priests, or the worship helpers, could go inside and meet with God. But when all the people saw the tabernacle, they'd think, *God is right here with us!*

Today we don't need a tabernacle or any other place for God to live in. Why? Because God sent the Holy Spirit to live inside our hearts! That means God is with us all the time.

God, thank You for wanting to be close
to Your people and close to me.

TRY it OUT

Set up your own tent or fort using a camping tent or blankets and furniture. Put things that are special to you inside it. Then make it a meeting place where you can talk with someone you love—maybe your parent or best friend—about important things. This is a bit like how the tabernacle was. It was a special place to meet with someone you love.

20

PSALM

noun \\'sä|m\\

a song or
poem that is a
prayer to God

If you could pick an emoji, or a little drawing of a face, to show how you have felt today, which one would you pick? Happy or sad? Excited or tired? Surprised or worried? Maybe you've even felt *all* of those—and more—at different times today!

Everybody has lots of feelings day after day, and there's a book in the Bible that proves we can share all those feelings with God. That book is called Psalms, and it's made up of a bunch of poems and songs—150 of them. Many people say it's their favorite book in the Bible because there are psalms that fit with just about any feeling you can imagine having.

God's people used these poems and songs to share their hearts with God and worship Him, and we can too! They are examples for us to follow.

King David wrote about half of the prayers in the book of

FiND It

IN THE BIBLE

PSALM 91

We don't know who wrote Psalm 91, but it sounds like they were in a dangerous situation—maybe a soldier about to go into battle. He wrote, "Being with God is like finding a safe place, a shelter where I can rest." When he was with God, he felt like he was in a strong tower where nothing could hurt him. He said, "God will protect me, like a bird covering her babies with her wing." Can you imagine how baby birds feel when they're all snuggled up to their mommy? God wants us to feel like that with Him. So just like the psalmist, we can say, "God, I trust in You. Keep me safe and close to You!"

Psalms. He talked to God about *everything*. Sometimes he would look up to the hills and cry out to God by saying, "I need help!" Other times he would say, "I'm scared!" or "I messed up!" Sometimes he'd cry and say, "God, I feel sadder than ever right now."

Other times David was exploding with joy. He'd shout, "God, You are *awesome*!" He'd play his harp and sing, "Thank You for everything!" Or he'd whisper, "I love You more than anything, God."

You know what? God wants you to do the same thing. He loves hearing you talk and sing to Him—about anything and everything!

~~~~~~~~~~~~~~~~~~

God, I'm so glad I can tell You anything.
I praise You for being so wonderful!

TRY it OUT

Come up with your own poem or song you can use as a prayer. Talk to God about anything on your mind or anything you love about Him. Or instead, just pick a worship song and sing it to God at bedtime.

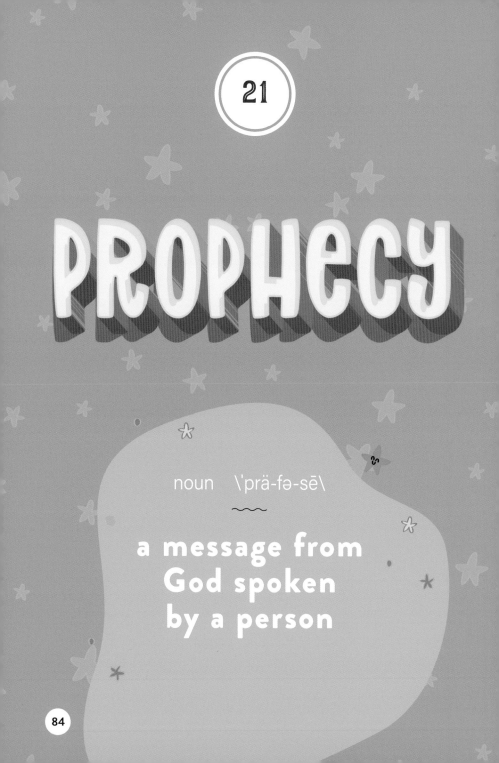

21

PROPHECY

noun \ˈprä-fə-sē\

a message from
God spoken
by a person

W e're meeting at the big tree at recess. Pass it on!" If someone said that to you, you'd be getting a special message. And when you passed it on, you'd be the messenger, the one giving the message.

God gave special messages that were called *prophecies*, and He picked certain people to become His prophets, or His messengers. These people would speak God's words to the rest of the people.

God reminded them, "I rescued you from slavery and made you My own special people. Don't you remember?" The Israelites had been acting like they'd forgotten all about God! They disobeyed Him all the time.

Has your teacher ever warned you that you'd get a punishment if you kept breaking a rule? That's kind of like what God was doing. He wanted to help the Israelites change. "Your sin will bring you trouble," God said. "But if you stop disobeying Me, I'll forgive you, and we can be close again."

FiND It

IN THE BIBLE

ISAIAH 35; LUKE 7:21-22

The prophet Isaiah told people that the coming Savior would do miracles—awesome things that showed God's power. These miracles wouldn't only amaze people—they'd also help them. Isaiah said, "He will make blind people see again and deaf people hear again. He will make people who normally can't walk jump like deer. He will make people who normally can't talk shout with joy." Hundreds of years later, Jesus did all of those things!

Some of the prophecies were about the future. "Just wait," a prophet would say, "someday God will send a mighty King who will rescue people from their sins."

The prophet Micah said, "This new king will be born in Bethlehem." Do you remember where Jesus was born? Bethlehem!

The prophet Isaiah said, "This Savior will die right next to criminals." And Jesus did that too.

After Jesus died and came back to life, He met with His followers and explained "what all the prophets had said about him" (Luke 24:27 ICB). It had all happened exactly as they'd said it would!

God, thank You for showing us Your love by speaking to us.

TRY it OUT

God still uses people to share His messages today. You can pass along God's messages from the Bible to others. Write out a Bible verse on a note card (for example, Ephesians 4:32). Then give that note card to a friend.

REDEMPTION

noun   \ri-'dem(p)-shən\

the act of buying back

What's your favorite thing you own? Imagine you lose it. Then someone finds it and says, "I'll let you have it back if you pay me twenty dollars." They're saying you'll have to pay for it to own it again.

When Jesus died on the cross, He paid a price to get us back too.

In the beginning, people belonged to God, but then they pulled away from Him and sinned. Their sin separated them from Him.

Our sin separates us from God too. And sin makes us its slaves. That means we can't stop wanting to do wrong things. It's like sin is our mean slave master who controls us and wants to keep us apart from God forever.

But God made a way to free us and get us back from sin. Because God is just, He wouldn't pretend like we hadn't done wrong things. He'd free us from sin while also keeping things right

FiND It

IN THE BIBLE

RUTH 3–4

When Ruth moved to a new town with her mother-in-law, Naomi, they had no money. But they found one of Naomi's relatives named Boaz. According to the law, Boaz could be Ruth's "family redeemer." The law said that if anyone was in trouble, the family redeemer should step in and help. That's what Boaz did! He used his own money to buy back the land that belonged to their family. He married Ruth and took care of her and Naomi.

and fair. That meant *redeeming* us—paying the price to buy us back from sin's hold on us. That price was Jesus' life.

It's like that mean slave master put us in a cage and said, "Ha! You'll never be free again." Then suddenly God showed up and handed over the payment to free us. God said to the slave master, "You don't own them anymore. I've paid the price, and they belong to Me now!"

God, thank You for redeeming me—for paying
the price to set me free from sin.

TRY it OUT

Go to an ice cream shop, and hand over the money to buy your ice cream yourself. That is just a little bit like how Jesus' life was given to buy back His people.

23

RESURRECTION

noun \ˌre-zə-ˈrek-shən\

coming back
to life
after dying

Who is your favorite superhero? Think of a time when that superhero was in trouble and it looked like the enemy was going to win. Then—surprise! The superhero used a burst of power to beat the enemy and save the day.

Jesus' resurrection was something like that. Who were the enemies? Satan, sin, and death. Who won? Well, when Jesus died, it looked like His enemies had won. But then—surprise! Jesus resurrected. That means He came back to life! He proved He was the most powerful and beat those enemies for good.

Jesus won the victory not only for Himself but for everyone who belongs to Him. It's like whoever believes in Jesus is on His

FiND It

MATTHEW 28:1–10

Three days after Jesus died, Mary and Mary Magdalene went to His tomb. All of a sudden, there was an earthquake, and a bright, shining angel appeared. The angel rolled away the big stone in front of Jesus' tomb so the women could see inside. He said, "Jesus is not here. He has risen from the dead, just like He said He would." The women ran to tell other people, and then they saw Jesus Himself! They were so amazed and happy. They bowed down, touched His feet, and worshiped Him.

team. He says to His team, "You're with Me. If I have won against those enemies, so have you."

Can you guess what that means? Someday everyone who believes in Jesus will come back to life, just like Jesus did! After we die, God will make us alive again. He will give us new bodies and bring us to heaven. All because we belong to the One who is the most powerful of all.

~~~~~~~~~~~~~~

God, thank You that I will come back to life like Jesus did!

TRY it OUT

The next time you're in a pool, hold a beach ball under the water, and then let go of it. What happens? It pops right up! It can't stay underwater. (You can try the same thing in a bathtub with an empty water bottle.) Jesus' power over sin and death is like that. The life in Him is stronger. God's power made Him rise up from the dead, and His power will do the same for us.

24

SALVATION

noun \sal-ˈvā-shən\

~~~~~

a rescue from
sin and a new
life with God

Imagine your mom buys tickets to see your favorite singer perform. You grab the tickets, shrieking with happiness. Later, at the concert, there's a person collecting tickets. You hand over your ticket, trusting it has the power to let you in—and it works!

This is kind of what it's like when God saves us. God "bought the tickets" for us by sending Jesus to die for our sins.

And then we need to do our part, which is believing in God. We need to reach out and grab the ticket—to show we trust in the power of what He's done. Just like you believe that your concert tickets will allow you to see your favorite singer, you know that believing in Jesus will allow you to see God in heaven.

The Bible says, "If you declare with your mouth, 'Jesus is Lord,'

FiND It

IN THE BIBLE

ACTS 10–11

Cornelius was a Roman officer—not part of the family of Israel. God told Peter, one of Jesus' disciples, to tell Cornelius how he could be saved through Jesus. God wanted Peter to learn that everyone— even people who weren't related to the Israelites—could be saved. Peter explained all of this to Cornelius and said, "Everyone who believes in Jesus will be forgiven." Then Cornelius believed and was saved!

and believe in your heart that God raised him from the dead, you will be saved. . . . Everyone who calls on the name of the Lord will be saved" (Romans 10:9, 13 NIV). It's really that simple!

As soon as we put our faith in Jesus, we're forgiven, and we're made righteous. That's when God gets rid of the sin separating us from Him.

Being saved isn't just about going to heaven one day. It changes how we live right now! We can get to know God better every day, and that makes our hearts happy. He shows us the best ways to live and makes us strong. He brings lots of love and joy to our lives!

God, I believe that what Jesus did for me saves me.

TRY it OUT

Pour some water in a bowl and sprinkle a bunch of pepper in it. Then put some liquid dish soap on your finger. Now touch the middle of the water's surface with that finger. What happens? The pepper rushes away! That is a picture of how God's power removes our sins.

25

SANCTIFICATION

noun   \ˌsaŋ(k)təfəkāshən\

~~~

the process of becoming holier

Let's say you've got a blank sheet of paper and some paintbrushes and paint. What would you do with that? You'd make something awesome, wouldn't you? You'd take your time and keep working until your painted picture was finished.

When God saves us from sin, His Spirit starts working on our hearts, just like painting a really awesome picture. He wants us to become more and more holy, like He is, and He won't stop working until His work in us is finished.

On our own, we are selfish and only care about getting what we want. But God changes our hearts so that we love what is good and want what He wants.

FiND It

IN THE BIBLE

LUKE 19:1-8

Zacchaeus's job was to gather people's money for paying taxes. He was sneaky and greedy, though—he took extra money from people so he could get rich. But when Zacchaeus met Jesus, he decided he wanted something better than sneaking and stealing. He said, "I won't do that anymore. I'll give back what I took—no, four times that! And I'll give half of my money to the poor!" God was working on Zacchaeus's heart to make him holier—and that's called sanctification!

We do our part by choosing to obey. Instead of just going along with whatever our friends are doing, we'll think, *What does God say about this?* We'll find out by reading the Bible. We'll pray, *God, help me follow You.*

Life on earth is getting us ready for something. Can you guess what that might be? For living in heaven! Heaven is a holy place. Each time we obey, we become more like Jesus, more like people who will be at home in heaven.

But when we mess up, God won't give up on us. The Bible tells us, "God began doing a good work in you. And he will continue it until it is finished"—in heaven (Philippians 1:6 ICB).

~~~~~~~~~~~~~~~~~

God, thank You for making me holy like You!

TRY it OUT

With a parent's help, get a piece of foil that is as wide as your shoulders. Close your eyes, then slowly and gently press the foil onto your face until it is touching every part of your face like a mask. Carefully pull it off and see what it looks like. Your face changed the shape of the foil—so it looks like you—just like God changes us to be like Him.

26

GOSPEL

noun \'gä-spəl\

the good news
of salvation
through Jesus

Yes," your mom says, "you can go ride roller coasters with your best friends next weekend."

You yell, "Yay!" and then run to tell your best friends the good news.

The disciples had some really good news too, and they couldn't wait to share it with others.

You see, the prophets had written that God would save people, but no one understood how He'd do it—not until after Jesus lived, died, and came back to life. Then the disciples understood God's plan. God was saving people through Jesus! And it was their job to share that good news with the world.

The gospel is the good news of God's amazing love for people and His big rescue plan. It's God's whole story in the Bible! He created everyone and reaches out to save them when they're in

FiND It

IN THE BIBLE

ACTS 8

An angel sent a man named Philip to travel on a road where he met an Ethiopian officer. He was in a chariot reading the words of a prophet. The Ethiopian said, "I need someone to explain this. Who is the prophet talking about?" Philip answered, "Jesus!" and explained the good news about Jesus. The Ethiopian started believing in Jesus. Then Philip baptized him, and the Ethiopian continued on his way home, full of joy because he had heard—and believed—the good news.

trouble. He says, "I'll help you and forgive you. I'll make you mine and give you life forever because I love you."

The good news is that you don't have to be good enough to be saved. It doesn't matter if you've broken rules before. Anyone can have a relationship with God and live with Him in heaven one day—you just have to believe in Jesus, ask God to forgive your sins, and follow Him.

Want to know a short way to explain the gospel? Just say John 3:16: "God loved the world so much that he gave his only Son. God gave his Son so that whoever believes in him may not be lost, but have eternal life" (ICB).

God, thank You for loving me and saving me! The gospel really is good news. Help me to share it with others!

TRY it OUT

Make a bracelet with six different colored beads with each color as a symbol of God's story of salvation: black for sin, red for Jesus' blood, white for forgiveness, blue for baptism, green for growth, and gold for eternal life. If anyone asks you about your bracelet, you can share the good news!

27

CONFESS

verb \kən-ˈfes\

to admit the wrong things we've done

I magine you're sick with a bad cough. Your mom offers you some cough medicine, but you pretend you're fine. As you keep playing, your cough gets worse . . . and worse. Finally, you admit it: you'll only get better if you take the medicine.

Confessing our sins is a lot like that. It's only when we admit to God we've done something wrong that we can get the "medicine" we need. And that medicine is forgiveness.

There was a time when King David kept pretending he hadn't done wrong things, but that only made him feel worse. He couldn't stop thinking about those bad things he'd done. "Finally," he said to God, "I confessed all my sins to you and stopped trying to hide my guilt. . . . And you forgave me! All my guilt is gone" (Psalm 32:5 NLT). David felt so much better after that!

FiND It
IN THE BIBLE

LUKE 15:11–24

One time a young man ran away from home after hurting his father's feelings. He spent his father's money on fun things. Then he ran out of money and started feeling alone, sad, and hungry. He decided to go back home. He knew he'd have to confess the wrong things he'd done—to be brave enough to tell the truth. The son said to his father, "I've sinned against God and against you. I'm sorry!" The father gave him a huge hug and said, "I thought I'd lost you. I'm so happy you're back! Let's have a party to celebrate!"

When we confess our sins, we're agreeing with God about what sin is. It's like we're saying, "If You say it's wrong, I agree it's wrong too."

We're also admitting *we* did that wrong thing. Sometimes it's really hard to do that, isn't it? But it's only when we get honest that things can get better.

~~~~~~~~~~

God, I admit that I've done wrong things,
like _____ . Thank You for forgiving me.

TRY it OUT

Put on a pair of dark sunglasses, then take them off. How different do things look when you take them off? Maybe with the sunglasses on, a blueberry looks black. Before we confess our sins, it's like we're wearing those sunglasses. We're not seeing things as they really are. We're telling ourselves we've done nothing wrong, but we're just pretending. When we confess, it's like taking off sunglasses. We can see what is true— what God has seen all along.

MERCY

noun \ˈmər-sē\

a choice to
not give the
punishment
someone
deserves

I magine you're in class and your teacher warns you that you will have to go see the principal the next time she catches you talking during reading time. A couple of minutes later, you start talking with a friend—again.

Suddenly your teacher sternly calls your name. Then she says, "Do you understand that you deserve to go see the principal?" You nod your head yes. "Well, today I'm going to give you mercy. You don't have to go to the principal. But let's really listen now, okay?"

This is how God treats us. We've done wrong things—we've hit our sister, lied to our dad, or hurt our friend's feelings. And it's like God has said, "Do you understand that you deserve punishment? Well, I'm deciding to give you mercy instead."

Do you remember what we said the punishment for sin is? It's being separated from God forever. But God wanted to rescue us from sin's punishment, so what did He do? He sent Jesus. Jesus

FiND It

IN THE BIBLE

LUKE 22:54–62; JOHN 21:15–19

After Jesus was arrested, one of His disciples, Peter, was embarrassed that he'd been friends with Jesus. People asked him, "Weren't you one of Jesus' disciples?" Peter lied and said, "No! I don't even know Him." Afterward he felt so bad because he had told a lie. But after Jesus came back to life, Jesus didn't punish Peter by pushing him away. Jesus gave him mercy. He even gave something special to Peter—the important job of building the church!

took on our punishment by dying on the cross. He made a way for us to be forgiven and become friends with God again—*even though we sinned.* That is amazing!

Why does God give us this amazing mercy? Do we earn it somehow? No! He gives it because of who He is. He gives it because He is good and gentle and kind.

And here's one more awesome thing: God doesn't get tired of giving mercy. The Bible tells us, "The Lord's love never ends. His mercies never stop. They are new every morning" (Lamentations 3:22–23 ICB). God keeps giving mercy to us *every single day.*

~~~~~~~~~~~~~~~~

God, thank You for giving me mercy!
Help me to give it to others too.

TRY it OUT

The next time others are mean to you, don't be mean back. Do something nice for them instead, like helping them on a project. Or if your brother has to do extra house cleaning as a punishment for something he did wrong, surprise him by helping him do it.

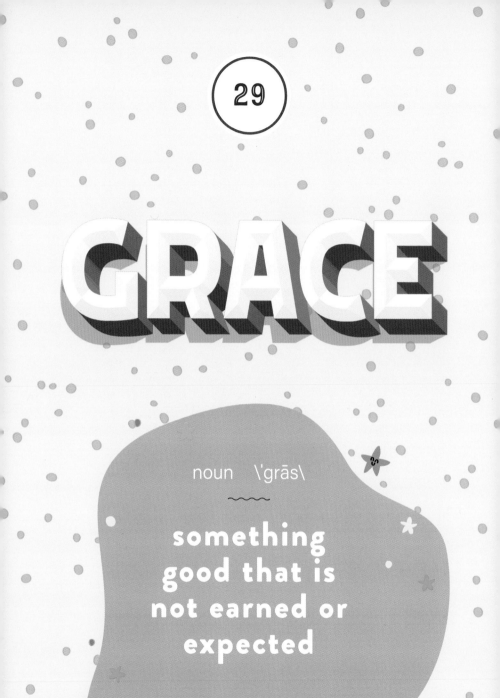

29

GRACE

noun   \'grās\

something
good that is
not earned or
expected

Let's say you're at your friend's house, and she decides to give you her favorite toy—just because. You didn't earn it or pay for it. It's not even your birthday or Christmas. She just wants to give you something good.

Grace is just like that. It's not a reward for meeting a goal or for doing good things. It's simply a gift, and the only reason for it is love.

God gives us gifts like this in all kinds of ways. To begin with, He created us! Since then, He has kept giving us what we need, along with all our favorite things—like chocolate, a cozy bed, playgrounds, and people who make us giggle. Every good thing in our lives is there because God wanted to give it.

He saves us from sin the same way. Romans 3:24 says, "People are made right with God by his grace, which is a free gift" (ICB).

FiND It

IN THE BIBLE

LUKE 10:25–37

Once a traveling Samaritan man came across a Jewish man who had been robbed and hurt. He was alone and so injured that he was close to dying. Even though most Samaritans and Jews hated each other, this Samaritan said, "I'm going to help you!" He bandaged up the hurt man and took him somewhere he could rest. He even paid other people to take care of the Jewish man. The Samaritan went out of his way to show grace.

Do you remember why we need this kind of gift? Because even if we always try to obey God, we eventually mess up. We could never do enough good things to "make up" for our sins. Grace—that good gift we can't earn—is the only way we can come close to God.

Sometimes grace seems too good to be true. But it *is* true because God really is that wonderful! Our job is to believe Him, to accept the good things He gives, and to love Him back. How do you think we can do that? By obeying Him and giving grace to others too!

God, thank You for the grace
You give me.

TRY it OUT

Offer a gift to your neighbors—not because it's their birthday or because it's Christmas but just because you want to be loving and kind. Maybe you could give them your favorite treat, or you could ask about helping with yard work. Do they need leaves raked or weeds pulled? Offer to do it for them, just as a gift.

FAITH

noun \ˈfāth\

being sure about
something you
cannot see,
touch, or hear

30

O h yeah? Prove it!"

Have you ever said that when someone claimed they could do something wild—maybe do the splits or juggle with their eyes closed? If you don't believe something until you see it, then you don't have faith.

One of Jesus' disciples, Thomas, didn't believe Jesus had risen from the dead. It wasn't until Thomas actually saw Jesus and His injuries from the cross that he believed. Maybe some of us would've done that too. But guess what—Jesus said it would've been better if Thomas had had *faith*, if he'd believed without having to see.

The Bible tells us, "Faith means being sure of the things we hope for. [It] means knowing that something is real even if we do not see it" (Hebrews 11:1 ICB). It's like if you're waiting for your mom

FiND It

IN THE BIBLE

LUKE 7:1–10

A Roman officer once asked Jesus to heal a sick person at his house. He showed his big faith in Jesus when he said, "You don't need to come into my house. . . . You only need to say the word, and my servant will be healed" (vv. 6–7 ICB). He believed in Jesus' power to do anything, wherever He was. Jesus was amazed! He said, "This is the greatest faith I have seen anywhere" (v. 9 ICB).

to pick you up from soccer practice. Even if she's a little late, you have faith that you'll see her soon.

If you have faith in God, it means that you believe He is real, even though you don't see Him. It means you believe God's love is strong, even though you can't always feel it. And it means you believe what God says in the Bible is true, even if you can't hear God's own voice.

So what do you think happens once we have faith in God? He'll forgive our sins. He'll make us strong. And He'll guide us as we live this fun adventure with Him each day.

God, I know You are real. I believe in Your love, and I trust everything You say.

TRY it OUT

Stand in front of a chair, facing away from it so it's behind you. Then—without touching or looking at it—bend down and sit in it. (That's probably something you do all the time!) Now think about it: you had faith that chair was there and would hold you up, even when you didn't see or touch it. You showed your faith by sitting in it.

31

DISCIPLE

noun   \dəˈsīpəl\

a student who
learns from and
becomes like
their teacher

If you want to learn how to play the piano, what do you do? First you need a piano and a teacher. Then you'll have to spend time with your teacher, listening to him and copying what he does. Before long you'll be able to play entire songs!

Jesus picked twelve people to be His special students—His disciples. They called Him "Teacher" and "Lord." The disciples spent all their time with Jesus and listened to everything He said. They watched how He loved God and helped people.

Jesus told His disciples, "Make God the most important thing in your life. And never act like you're more important than other people. Instead, *love* them. Find ways to serve them!" He gave them an example by washing their dirty, stinky feet. Do you think that was a smelly job? It sure was! But Jesus did it anyway.

FiND It
IN THE BIBLE

MATTHEW 4

Peter and Andrew were fishermen, and one day Jesus said to them, "Come, follow Me. I will make you fishers of men." That meant they'd start finding people who needed Jesus—instead of finding fish. Peter and Andrew didn't understand and probably wondered, *What exactly will we have to do? How will we do it?* But they trusted Jesus without having it all figured out. They stopped fishing and started following Jesus, making Him the most important person in their lives.

"Show God and people that you love them by copying what I do," Jesus said. And so—just like you would copy your piano teacher—the disciples started doing what Jesus did.

Jesus wants us to be His disciples too. We can't see and hear Him like the first disciples did, but we can still get close to Him. Can you guess how we can do that? By praying, reading the Bible, and being around other Christians. We'll learn to obey Him, even when it's hard, and treat other people the same way we want to be treated. The more we love Jesus and stay close to Him, the more we'll want to follow Him.

Jesus, thank You for letting me be Your disciple! Teach me to be like You.

TRY it OUT

Play follow-the-leader with some friends. The leader will walk around a playground or backyard. Maybe she'll do some big jumps or goofy wiggles! Everyone else will go wherever the leader takes them and follow all her fun moves. That's what we do as Jesus' disciples—we follow Him wherever He leads. We do what He does.

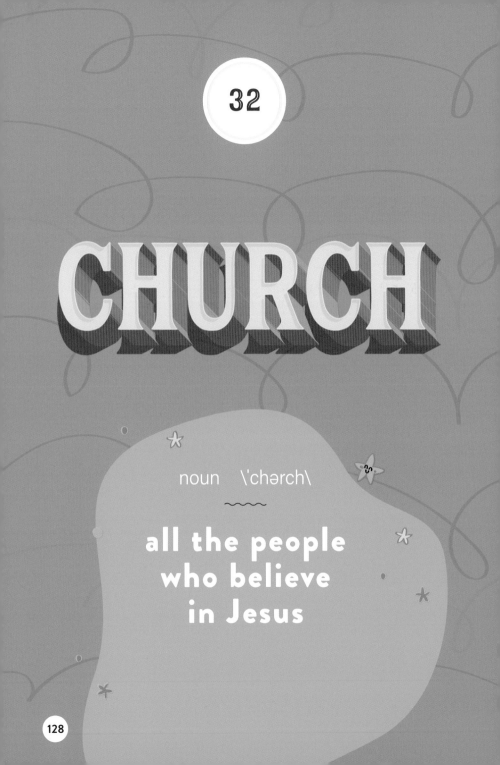

32

CHURCH

noun \\'chərch\\

all the people
who believe
in Jesus

Imagine you *love* to jump rope. Then you find out the coolest thing ever: a jump rope club just started at your school—and you can join! Every week you get to do your favorite activity with other people who love it too. Not only do you get to practice and learn more jump rope tricks, but you also get to make new friends.

When you put your faith in Jesus, you get to join a group of people who are involved with the best club ever—the church!

The Bible describes the church as a group of people, not as a building. After Jesus went back to heaven, everyone who believed in Him started meeting with other people who believed. Those meetings became known as church services. Now, many years later, we do the very same thing.

FiND It

IN THE BIBLE

ACTS 3–4, 9, 16, 18

The early church worked like a team to show love to people and provide what they needed. Joseph sold a field and then gave all the money to people in need. Tabitha made clothes for people. Lydia and Priscilla both invited people into their homes. The disciples taught about Jesus and healed people. They were all continuing what Jesus had been doing, and many more people joined God's family because of them.

When we meet with other people who believe in God, we get to do something really special. Do you know what it is? We get to come closer to God! How do we do that? By worshiping Him together. We sing and celebrate who God is. We thank Him and say, "Wow!" about all He has done. We learn more about Him and His best ways for living. We take communion and talk to God together in prayer. We also help each other with problems and encourage each other.

All of this helps us stay connected to God and to each other.

When we do that, we can live like Jesus and show His love and goodness to the world. Then even more people will get to know Jesus and join God's family too.

~~~~~~~~~~~~~~~~~~

God, thank You for making me part of Your family, the church!

TRY it OUT

The Bible says the world is dark but God is light, and the church is supposed to share God's light. Take a flashlight into a dark room with no sunlight, and then turn on the flashlight. Doesn't that make a huge difference? That's what it's like when you show Jesus to the world!

33

BAPTISM

noun \ˈbap-ˌti-zəm\

a special act
using water
that shows
we've joined
God's family

Before you start a new school year or go to camp, you need to write your name on everything you take with you. Why? So everyone can tell who each backpack or pillow or baseball belongs to.

Getting baptized shows that we belong to Jesus and God's family, the church. It's something we do to "act out" being connected to Jesus—we're connected to His dying and coming back to life. What does that mean? Well, Jesus' death paid the punishment for our sins, so now we're forgiven because we're *connected to Him*. And someday we'll come back to life just like He did because we're *connected to Him*. Isn't that awesome?

The special act of baptism is also a way to show people that we're making an important decision—that we're saying no to sin and yes to obeying God's best ways to live.

Getting baptized is like shouting from the rooftops, "I'm a

FiND It

IN THE BIBLE

ACTS 16; MATTHEW 28:19

When Paul and Silas were in prison, God brought an earthquake to open the jail doors. When the jailer saw that Paul, Silas, and the other prisoners hadn't tried to escape, he was shocked! Then he listened as Paul and Silas explained how Jesus saves people. He started believing in Jesus, and right away he was baptized. Then the same thing happened with his whole family. Paul and Silas were obeying Jesus' command to help people all over the world become His followers and to baptize them into God's family.

Christian now! I'm part of this family of love and forgiveness! I'm going to live with joy, peace, and hope!"

Baptisms look different in different churches. Some baptize babies; others wait until people are older. Some sprinkle water on a person's head; others put their whole body under water. Either way, the water shows that our sins have been washed away.

But there's one thing that happens in every Christian baptism: we baptize people "in the name of the Father and the Son and the Holy Spirit" (Matthew 28:19 ICB).

<hr />

God, thank You for this special way to show
people I'm part of Your family.

TRY it OUT

Get matching bracelets for you and your best friends, and wear them every day. Or use a stamp to mark the hand of each of your family members. Then take a picture of all your stamped hands together. Doing things like this shows that you belong to each other in a special way—kind of like baptism!

COMMUNION

noun \kə-ˈmyü-nyən\

the acts of
receiving and
remembering
Jesus by eating
bread and
drinking wine

What's your favorite food? Maybe pizza or macaroni and cheese? Maybe cookies or ice cream? Imagine that your neighbor surprises you with that food. Would you set it aside and ignore it? No, you'd start munching on it. You'd accept that nice gift and put it right into your belly.

Well, Jesus gave us the most special gift ever—the gift of Himself. Do you remember that He died so that our sins could be forgiven? That means Jesus gave His life for us! And when we believe in Him, we accept His amazing gift.

Communion is a way for us to remember Jesus and how He gave His life for us. Do you know how communion started? Jesus did it first with His disciples. He gave them bread to eat and wine to drink and said, "This bread is My body that I'm giving for you.

FiND It

IN THE BIBLE

---

1 CORINTHIANS 11

The first followers of Jesus took communion often, but after a while some of them started doing it wrong. They'd bring a big loaf of bread and gobble it up while another person was still hungry. And they wouldn't share! They could only think about themselves—they weren't feeling close to Jesus and others. So Paul said, "Make sure everyone gets a chance to eat the bread and drink the wine. Don't forget, communion is all about Jesus and His love." After all, Jesus had said, "Do this to remember Me" (1 Corinthians 11:24 ICB).

This wine is My blood that I'm giving for you." This happened the night before Jesus died, so He was saying, "I'm giving you *My life*. Accept this gift from Me." And that's exactly what the disciples did when they ate the bread and drank the wine.

Christians today do the same thing with other believers. In communion we all come close to Jesus and feel His love. We remember what He did for us, and we offer Him a thankful heart.

~~~~~~~~~~~~~~~~~

Jesus, I accept Your love and the gift of Yourself. I love You back!

TRY it OUT

Choose a healthy snack, then ask an adult to help you research what nutrients that food has. How does it help your body? Maybe it makes your skin healthy or your muscles stronger. Then eat it as you think about how that food is helping and nourishing you. Receiving communion is like that—Jesus feeds your soul.

35

WITNESS

noun \\'wit-nəs\

~~~

someone who
sees or hears
about something
and then tells
others about it

Who is someone famous you'd like to meet? If you met that person, what would you do? You'd probably get super excited and then tell everyone you know all about it!

As God's children, we know about something really exciting. We know that Jesus gave up His life for us so our sins could be forgiven, and now we can be close with God. That's amazing! It changes everything for us. It means we have a bright future to look forward to and that we belong in God's happy family.

That's a way bigger deal than meeting someone famous, isn't it? So of course we want to tell people all about it!

Well, that's exactly what Jesus told His followers to do after He came back to life. He said, "You saw what happened—you are witnesses. Now go tell everyone about God's love and forgiveness!"

FiND It

IN THE BIBLE

ACTS 4

Two of Jesus' followers, Peter and John, were sharing the good news about Jesus' love and forgiveness with a lot of people. Thousands of people started believing in Jesus because of them! But telling people about Jesus was against the rules at the time, so Peter and John were put in jail. They didn't mind! They said, "We're obeying God by telling people what is true. We can't keep quiet about what we've seen and heard—about how amazing God is!"

Since then, people have been sharing God's message so everyone in the world can hear about it. They've been *witnessing* to others about what they know about Jesus.

How do you think we could do that too? By explaining to others what we've learned from the Bible about Jesus. Or by showing God's love to them—by doing something kind or taking care of them somehow. We've found out how wonderful God is, and we want others to find out too. We want to help them join God's happy family however we can.

~~~~~~~~~~

God, I want to help other people have what You've given me— love, forgiveness, joy, and hope. Help me be a witness for You.

TRY it OUT

Line up some dominoes, then knock down the first one so it moves all the others. When you are a witness of God's love, you're like that first domino reaching another domino. You reach one person you know with God's message, then that person reaches someone else, and it just keeps going. You do your part by telling the people you know about Jesus.

OBEDIENCE

noun \ō-ˈbē-dē-ən(t)s\

the act of doing what God says to do

magine you're walking your dog and he starts snarling at another dog. He even tries to bite him. "Stop! No!" you yell, but your dog won't listen. He almost hurts the other dog before you pull him away. Afterward you start teaching him not to do that anymore. Eventually he learns to obey.

You know better than your dog about what is good, don't you? Well, God knows better than we do about what's good. We need to listen to Him—instead of doing whatever we feel like doing—because He knows the best ways to live.

When God gives us commands, He's helping us, like a good teacher. And when we obey Him, He brings us good things. Like if you forgive a friend, you'll feel closer to that friend. Or if you always tell the truth to your parents, they'll trust what you say and be proud of you.

FiND It

IN THE BIBLE

DANIEL 3

Shadrach, Meshach, and Abednego lived in a kingdom where the king commanded everyone to worship a statue of him. These three men loved God and knew it would be wrong to worship anyone but Him. But the king said anyone who didn't worship the statue would be put into a fiery furnace. Shadrach, Meshach, and Abednego said, "Our God can save us. But even if He doesn't, we won't disobey Him by worshiping that statue." So they went into that furnace, but God protected them. The flames didn't touch them, and they came out alive!

Remember that we don't obey God so we can be saved. We obey God to show Him we love Him! It's our way to worship Him and prove we trust Him.

Is it hard to obey God sometimes? Yes. We may be the only ones doing it, other people may put us down, or we'd rather do something more fun. But when God is most important to us, we'll want to obey anyway. And if we have trouble obeying, we can ask God to help us—and He will!

———————————

God, I trust You and want to always obey You.

TRY it OUT

Ask an adult to help you bake cookies from scratch. You'll have to follow the rules carefully. What if you put in a cup of salt instead of a cup of sugar? It would taste terrible! What if you forgot the flour and baking powder? It would become a big, messy blob! But when you follow the directions, you get some delicious, gooey cookies. Obeying God is just like that—life is best when we do things His way.

37

TEMPTATION

noun   \tem(p)-ˈtā-shən\

a feeling of
being pulled
toward doing
something bad

P ull harder!" someone shouts. You're in a line of people gripping a rope in a game of tug-of-war. The other team is pulling your team toward them, but you want to stop them. You use all your strength to pull back the other way.

A tug-of-war is like temptation—you're feeling pulled toward sin, and you have to fight back.

Everyone struggles with wanting to sin, with wanting to do something wrong. Maybe you've wanted to lie to avoid getting in trouble, or you've wanted to be mean to someone who has hurt you. It may not feel like it, but you always have a choice—you can always choose to do what's right.

You might wonder, *Is temptation a hard, mean test from God?* Absolutely not! It's our own bad desires that make us tempted. God is never on the other side of the rope, pulling us toward sin. He hates sin! He is on our side of the rope, moving us away from sin.

FiND It

IN THE BIBLE

MATTHEW 4:1–10

While Jesus was in the desert for forty days, Satan kept tempting Him to do wrong things. Each time Jesus fought back by speaking words from the Bible. Satan said, "Prove you're God's Son by falling from a tall building and then making Him rescue You." Jesus replied, "No! Scripture says, 'Do not test God.'" Satan told Jesus, "Worship me," and Jesus said, "No! Scripture says, 'Only worship God.'" The power of God's words about what is right and good helped Jesus escape temptation every time.

First Corinthians 10:13 says that God "will not let you be tempted more than you can stand. But when you are tempted, God will also give you a way to escape that temptation" (ICB).

God can make you strong enough to fight back—to walk away from a tempting situation or put your mind on something else. He might remind you of a Bible verse, something good and true you can focus on instead. He doesn't expect you to beat temptation on your own! Any time you feel tempted, you can ask God to help you do the right thing.

~~~~~~~~~~~~~~~~~~~

God, thank You for helping me say no to sin.

TRY it OUT

Push two magnets together so that they come close to snapping together. That pull between them is like when you are tempted to sin. Now turn them so that one magnet pushes away the other one. That's like God's power helping you push away sin.

38

PRIDE

noun \ˈprīd\

the thought that you're better than you are or more important than others

I bet I'm the best climber here," a classmate says at recess near the big tree. "Get out of the way! I'm going first!" He starts pushing his way through the other kids.

"It's not your turn," you call out. But the boy pushes to the front and tries to climb the tree—but he can't jump high enough to reach the first branch! Yikes.

You might say this boy was proud in a selfish way, which the Bible says is bad. It's different from having confidence—being sure we can do something—and from the good kind of pride, like when we've worked hard on a project and feel happy about it.

Selfish pride is all about being focused on ourselves. We say, "Look at me!" or "I'm the best!" We always push to get our way. We never say, "I'm sorry" or admit our mistakes.

If we act this way, do you think people will like being around us? No! And we'll probably end up hurting or embarrassing ourselves

FiND It

IN THE BIBLE

DANIEL 4

King Nebuchadnezzar was very proud of his power. He didn't care about avoiding sin or pleasing God or anyone else. He was cruel to people and told them to worship him. Eventually God said, "You don't get to be king anymore—or even *speak*. You must leave the kingdom and live with wild animals until you change your ways." Nebuchadnezzar started eating grass like a cow, and his nails grew so long that they looked like bird claws. No kidding! Since Nebuchadnezzar wouldn't humble himself, God put him in a situation that *made* him humble.

somehow—just like the boy who couldn't reach the branch on the tree.

Here's something even worse about pride: it leads us to sin. We get so focused on what we want and what we can do that we end up thinking, *I can be good without God. I don't need His help.*

So God tells us, "Be humble." That means *not* thinking we're the most important person in the world. Instead, we know that God is the most important. We think about what other people need and feel. We let others go first in line. And we encourage and help them!

~~~~~~~~~~~

God, You are the most important. I want to do things Your way, and I know I need Your help!

TRY it OUT

Chew some gum, and try to blow some bubbles. Once you get a big, strong bubble, what happens? It pops! Let's say the gum is like people and the air inside the bubble is like pride. Getting puffed up with pride leads to trouble, just like a bubble growing bigger and then going *pop!*

PHARISEE

noun   \ˈfarəˌsē\

a Jewish leader
focused on
following rules

39

Have you ever done something good for the wrong reason? Maybe you're nice to your brother when your mom's watching, but you're sometimes mean when she isn't. You're being nice only because you want to look good in front of your mom.

The Pharisees were kind of like that. They'd do good things, like pray, in front of people to get noticed—not because they really loved God. They actually thought they were right with God just because they followed a bunch of rules—rules from God's law, plus their own rules about how to please God. They were very proud of themselves and wouldn't admit to doing anything wrong.

Most people were amazed at how much the Pharisees obeyed God, but almost no one could see that their hearts didn't love

FiND It

IN THE BIBLE

LUKE 18:11–14

Jesus once told a story about a proud Pharisee who stood tall and prayed, "God, I thank you that I'm not as bad as other people" (v. 11 ICB). Then another man beat on his chest to show he was sad. He prayed, "God, have mercy on me. I am a sinner!" (v. 13 ICB). He wasn't too proud to say how much he needed God. And so, Jesus said, the second man was made right with God.

God. The Pharisees would secretly "cheat widows and steal their homes" and then "try to make themselves look good by saying long prayers" (Mark 12:40 ICB).

On the outside, they looked good. But on the inside? Not so much. It was like if you grabbed a banana that looked perfect, but the inside was rotten when you peeled it. Jesus told the Pharisees, "You may say things that honor God, but you don't really mean it. You don't have love for God in your heart."

A lot of "acting good" can never make us right with God— that can only happen when we trust in Jesus. God wants us to obey Him because we love Him, not to look good.

God, I want to be honest about my sins
and obey You with a loving heart.

TRY it OUT

Create a face mask out of paper, cutting out holes for eyes and drawing a big smile on it. Now put it on your face and look in the mirror. Make a mad face under the mask. When we do good things only to get noticed, not because we care, we're just putting on a show. It's like putting on a mask and pretending to be something we're not.

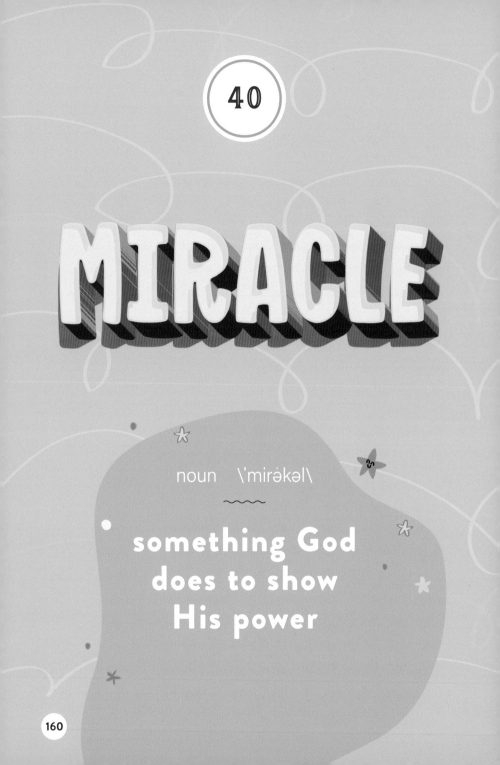

40

MIRACLE

noun \ˈmirəkəl\

something God
does to show
His power

Have you ever seen a magic trick that amazed you—like a rabbit being pulled out of a hat? Magic tricks get our attention because something surprises us. We see something happen that we didn't expect or didn't think could happen and say, "Whoa!"

Jesus did amazing things too—but He didn't do tricks. He performed miracles. When He was at a wedding and the hosts ran out of wine, He turned water into wine. When thousands of hungry people had no food, He made a bunch of food appear, and everyone got plenty. When He met blind, paralyzed, or sick people, He healed them. He even brought dead people back to life!

Why do you think Jesus did these miracles? Well, He wanted to help and take care of people. He also wanted everyone to see

FiND It

IN THE BIBLE

JOHN 11:1–44

Jesus' friend Lazarus was so sick that he was about to die. Someone asked Jesus to come quickly to heal Lazarus. Jesus didn't come right away, though, because He had a special plan. By the time He arrived, Lazarus had been dead for several days, and all his friends were so sad. Then Jesus surprised everyone by calling out toward Lazarus's tomb, "Lazarus, come out!" (v. 43 ICB). And Lazarus did! Jesus proved that He was more powerful than death.

His power and believe that He was God's Son. No one but God could do the things He did. That includes forgiving sins and coming back to life after He died on the cross. Those are the most amazing miracles of all!

Just think about how God used His power to create the whole world. Now think about how each miracle Jesus did gave people a peek at God's power. It's the same power He can use at *any time* to do *anything*! Seeing His power helps us trust Him more and know He will take care of us.

~~~~~~~~~~~~

God, there is no one as powerful as You! Thank You for the miracles You've done.

TRY it OUT

Find a toy that uses batteries. With your parents' help, take the batteries out, and try playing with it. You might find a way to have fun with it, but it's not doing what it's supposed to be doing, is it? Now put the batteries back in and turn it on. *Ta-da!* Now you see it's got power. Something is making it move, make sounds, or light up. It's the same way with miracles—they show God's power.

41

noun \ˈpa-rə-bəl\

a story that
teaches a truth
about God

Do you like riddles? See if you can answer these: What goes up but never comes down? What's something that belongs to you but others use more than you do? And what is as big as a giraffe but weighs nothing? (*Look for the answers at the bottom of this section.*)

Jesus told stories called *parables*, and they were kind of like riddles because they really made people think. Some people who heard them just scratched their heads and said, "Huh?" These stories seemed like weird brain teasers to them.

But other people who were listening carefully realized something amazing: Jesus' parables had hidden messages! They revealed important truths about God—how things work in His kingdom and why Jesus came to earth. It was kind of like figuring out the answer to a riddle.

One parable was about a man who had one hundred sheep.

FiND It

IN THE BIBLE

MATTHEW 20:1–16

One of Jesus' parables was about workers in a vineyard. Some of them worked a long time, while others worked a short time, but they were all paid the same amount of money. The workers who worked a long time said, "Hey, don't we deserve more money or some kind of special treatment?" But the person in charge said, "All that really matters is that I've decided to be generous to everyone." This parable meant that people who have believed in God for a long time aren't more important than new believers. *Everyone* in God's kingdom gets mercy! No one should act like they're better than anyone else.

Boy, did he love those sheep! One day one of the sheep went missing. Do you think the man said, "Oh well," and just forgot about that sheep? No way! He went looking for it. And when he found that lost sheep he loved, he was so thrilled. He probably did a happy dance!

What was the truth hidden inside this parable? That God doesn't want any of His children to be far away from Him. And that Jesus came to earth to bring them home, just like the shepherd in the story!

~~~~~~~~~~

God, I want to learn all about You and Your kingdom. Help me to understand each important truth in the Bible.

Answers: your age; your name; a giraffe's shadow

TRY it OUT

Put a fun surprise inside an envelope (maybe some stickers or a funny drawing) along with a note, and give it to a friend. When they see it, they'll think, *I wonder what's inside the envelope?* When they open it, they'll discover what it is. The same is true when we listen to Jesus' parables and learn what they mean.

WISDOM

noun   \ˈwiz-dəm\

the ability
to know and
do what God
says is right

This is so cool!" you shriek as you hold your new remote-controlled toy helicopter. You want to start playing with it, but you don't know how it works. How will you figure it out? By reading the instructions! Those are written by the people who made the toy.

God gives us something like instructions for life, and it's called *wisdom*. Wisdom comes from God because He made us and knows what's best for us.

Wisdom guides us in doing what's right and keeps us from making mistakes that hurt others and ourselves. It protects us and brings good things into our lives.

For example, God says it's wise to be careful about what we say. What would happen if you always talked back to your teacher and said mean things to your friends? You'd end up in trouble, and

FiND It

IN THE BIBLE

MATTHEW 7:24–27

Jesus told a story about two men building houses. One man was foolish and built a house on top of sand. As soon as a storm came, the house fell with a big *crash*. The other man was wise and built his house on a rock. His house stood strong in the storm. Jesus said that anyone who listens to His teaching and ignores it is foolish, like the man who used sand. But people who listen to Him and do what He says are wise, like the man who used rock.

your friends wouldn't want to hang out with you. But what if instead your words were respectful, kind, and loving? Well, then you'd have a lot of happiness and fun with your teacher and friends!

"Use wisdom," God says, "and it will take care of you. Love wisdom, and it will keep you safe. Wisdom is the most important thing" (Proverbs 4:6–7 ICB).

How do you think we can get wisdom? By reading the Bible and by just asking for it! The Bible says if we need wisdom, we should ask God for it, and He'll give it to us (James 1:5). He'll help us understand what really matters—what is true and best—as we make choices in life.

God, make me wise like You.

TRY it OUT

The next time you're watching a movie, see if you can spot anyone doing what God says is wise. Maybe they never say anything mean, even when they feel mad or sad. Maybe they work hard instead of being lazy. Maybe they listen to the advice of wise people instead of just doing whatever they want. Then see if you can spot something good that happens after people make wise choices.

43

PEACE

noun   \\'pēs\\

a state of living without fear or fighting

In your living room the TV is blaring, your sister is playing the guitar, and your brother is yelling, "Boom! Boom!" as he crashes toy cars into each other. The noise is super loud, but then you step outside the door. Ahhhh . . . it's so peaceful!

In the Bible, peace actually means more than just quiet. It can mean "complete or whole." It involves taking something broken or messed up and making it right—like how you would fix your neighbor's fence if your dog tore it down.

We can have several kinds of peace: peace with others, peace with God, and peace in our hearts.

Peace with others is when we get along with people. We don't fight, and we forgive each other when we mess up.

Peace with God is something we have through Jesus. After sin broke our relationship with God, Jesus made a way for our sins

FiND It

IN THE BIBLE

MATTHEW 8:23–27

One day when Jesus and His disciples were on a boat, a big storm hit. Waves started coming into their boat, and the disciples were really scared they would drown—especially since Jesus was asleep! After they woke Him up, Jesus commanded the wind and sea to become calm. *And they did.* Jesus showed that He has the power to bring peace to any situation, whether it's a wild storm or a frightened heart.

to be forgiven. He makes us right with God again—He brings peace to that relationship.

We can also receive God's gift of peace in our hearts. Everyone feels worried, scared, or angry sometimes, but Jesus says, "Don't be afraid. I will give you My peace. Trust in Me!"

When we feel upset, we can pray, "God, I'm worried about . . ." or "I'm scared of . . ." And you know what? We'll feel calmer. It's like feeling overwhelmed in a noisy room and then walking outside. We'll remember that God's power is bigger than everything, even our problems. And God will give us a peace that we can't even understand. It will become like a shield that protects our hearts and minds.

~~~~~~~~~~~~~~~~~~

God, thank You for bringing peace into my life.

TRY it OUT

In a pool, bathtub, or sink full of water, move your hands up and down in the water until you make big waves (just make sure you don't let water spill out). Then stop moving and be very still. The water will calm down and become still, just like how Jesus can bring you peace.

44

JOY

noun   \'joi\

~~~

a gladness
about God and
His goodness

Imagine having a bad day. A friend wasn't nice to you, you got hurt during a soccer game, and your team lost. You feel sad. But as you head home, you think about the good things you'll find there: parents who love you, a pet to play with, a yummy dinner, and a comfy blanket. You start to feel better. Although the bad stuff of the day isn't magically going away, the good stuff can still make you happy.

God's joy is kind of like that—we can have it anytime, no matter how bad things get. He always gives us reasons to be glad! He loves us and saves us from sin. He's strong and takes care of us. He made a beautiful world full of things to learn, places to explore, and people to enjoy. He's always with us and promises to take us to heaven.

Do those things go away when we feel sad? No! But God is good and wonderful all the time.

FiND It

IN THE BIBLE

PHILIPPIANS 1–4

Paul was put in prison for telling people about Jesus and how He could save them from their sins. Did Paul say, "I can't be happy anymore because I'm in prison. This is too awful!"? Nope. He kept thinking about God's love and the good things God had shown him. Paul said, "I can be sad but still have joy." He wrote letters to people, encouraging them to trust God and be joyful.

So God can give us joy, but how? Well, sometimes it comes when we notice good things around us. Like if you take a walk outside, and you think about how much you like what you see—colorful flowers, funny bugs, people to wave at—and you feel happy.

Other times we have joy when we pray or read the Bible. We thank God for good things and feel glad about being friends with Him. And if we still feel stuck without joy, we can ask God to give it to us.

And you know what? As we have more of God's joy in our hearts, we'll discover something else that's awesome: His joy makes us strong.

~~~~~~~~~~~~

God, You give me joy and make my heart happy!

TRY it OUT

Line up some big marshmallows in a row. Find some smooth rocks about the same shape and line them up too. Next, press down on the marshmallows as hard as you can, then do the same with the rocks. Those marshmallows got squished, but the rocks stayed the same. When we have God's joy, we're strong like those rocks. The hard things in life don't squish out that joy!

45

HOPE

verb   \'hōp\

looking forward
to good things
in the future

"Tomorrow is going to be awesome!" Have you ever said that before a super fun day? Maybe you were going to have a big birthday party, and you couldn't wait to see all your friends and share a birthday cake.

That excitement and happiness about what's ahead is called *hope*. Having hope in God means that we're looking forward to Him doing all the good things He has promised to do.

Why do we have hope? Is it because we have a cheerful personality? Nope. Is it because we can see signs that good things are coming—like how a flower bud on a branch shows spring is coming? No again. We have hope because we trust who God is. We trust whatever He says because He always tells the truth. And He has told us something really wonderful is coming.

First Peter 1:4 says, "Now we hope for the blessings God has for his children. These blessings are kept for you in heaven" (ICB).

FiND It

IN THE BIBLE

LUKE 8

A woman who had been sick for twelve years saw Jesus in a crowd of people. She had heard about His power. She thought, *If anything or anyone could heal me, it'd be Jesus.* And so, with hope in her heart, the woman walked closer to Him. When she was right behind Him, she touched His coat—just the edge of it. And guess what! As soon as she did that, Jesus' power healed her!

What are these blessings? They're a little crazy to imagine: We'll get to rise from the dead, just like Jesus did. We'll get to become like Him—holy, pure, and loving. We'll get to go to a new home in heaven, where we'll always feel God's love and be happy.

Basically, God is going to take everything that is wrong and make it right again. You know how a scrape on your knee goes away after it heals? God is going to heal the whole world from all the ways sin has hurt it. That means no one will ever be mean or make anyone feel sad or scared. Nothing will break, no one will get sick, and everyone will be friends. God says to us, "You can count on Me to make wonderful things happen. So get excited—you're going to love what I'll do!"

~~~~~~~~~~

God, my hope is in You. Thank You for giving me so much to look forward to!

TRY it OUT

Plant a seed in soil, then water it regularly. As you wait for it to grow, you are hoping—looking forward to seeing it bloom.

46

LOVE

verb   \'ləv\

wanting goodness for someone and working to bring it to them

I love pizza!" "I love this song!" "I love this game!"

We say we love things all the time, don't we? What we mean is that these things are fun, yummy, or our favorites. But God's way of loving means a whole lot more than that.

The Bible says that God *is* love. That means He is completely loving, and He shows us what real love is. Loving a song or food is nowhere near how big God's love is. If we tried to imagine the biggest thing in the world, God's love would be bigger. It goes on and on forever! Nothing can stop His love or keep us away from it.

That includes our sin. First John 4:9 says, "This is how God showed his love to us: He sent his only Son into the world to give us life through him" (ICB). We don't earn His love. He just gives it because of how much He cares for us.

God shows His love by giving us good things, and then He does even more: He puts His love *into* our hearts. Imagine God's love is

FiND It

IN THE BIBLE

RUTH 1–4

Naomi was so sad after her husband and her sons died. She had to move somewhere else and felt lonely. Ruth, the wife of one of Naomi's sons, said, "I'll go with you. I'll help you and be a friend to you forever." Ruth gave up her home and friends—everything that was familiar. When they got to the new place, Ruth worked in the fields to provide food for Naomi. She took care of Naomi and kept her promise to her—because she loved her!

a gigantic waterfall and your heart is a little cup. What would happen if that cup sat under the waterfall? It'd fill up—and overflow! When that love in our hearts overflows, we can give it away to others.

And how, exactly, do we do that? Maybe by sharing our lunch with a friend or cleaning up the kitchen after dinner. By saying, "I'm sorry" and "I forgive you." Or by encouraging the people around us and not giving up on them when things get hard.

Because God never gives up on us!

God, thank You for giving me Your wonderful love.

TRY it OUT

Set a cup inside a big baking pan. Then take a pitcher of water and pour water into the cup until it overflows. This is just like how God can fill our hearts with His love so much that it overflows, and then we can give it away.

47

WORKS

noun \\'wərks\

**the good things
we do that
please God**

Surprise!" you say, as you bring breakfast to your mom. She's still in bed and grinning at you. "You do so much for me," you say. "*I* wanted to do something for *you*."

When we have real love in our hearts, we'll show it in what we do. The same is true when we have real faith in God—we prove it by our actions.

Now, are we saved from our sins by doing good works? Is that how we're made right with God? No! We're saved only by God's grace. But once we join God's loving family, we *want* to do good things. Getting to know God changes us.

We'll want to make Him smile and be like Him. We'll want to bring food to the hungry, learn about the Bible, be patient with our sister, or help at church.

FiND It

IN THE BIBLE

MATTHEW 21:28–32

Jesus told a story about how important our actions are. A father told his two sons to work in his vineyard. The first son said, "I won't go," but later he realized that was wrong. So he went and did the work. The second son said to his father, "Yes, sir, I'll go work." But he never went! Jesus asked, "Which son obeyed his father?" The right answer was the first son. We show our love by what we do, not just what we say.

Ephesians 2:10 says, "In Christ Jesus, God made us new people so that we would do good works. God . . . had planned for us to live our lives doing them" (ICB). We were made to do these good things—just like paintbrushes were made for painting and playground swings were made for swinging.

These works also show the world what God is like. You can think of them like sparkling fireworks in the sky. They make the world brighter, and when people see them, they'll see how wonderful God is! And God will even use your good works to do a really big work He's doing—helping people to feel His love and become friends with Him.

~~~~~~~~~~

God, help me show my love and faith by doing things that make You smile.

TRY it OUT

Add food coloring to a glass of water, then put a stalk of celery in it. Let it sit overnight. The next morning the celery will have changed color! That colored water is like our love and faith—when it's in our hearts, it comes out in our actions. It changes what we do.

48

HONOR

verb \ˈä-nər\

showing
someone they're
important

What if you walked into your principal's office and started jumping on her desk and demanding some snacks? Would she like that? No way! It'd be rude and foolish to treat anyone that way, especially someone in charge. Whenever you're around your principal, what do you do instead? You honor her—which means you show her she's important—by listening to her and doing whatever she says.

The Bible tells us to honor God, our parents, and other people in charge by obeying them. It also tells us to honor *everyone*. That's a lot of people! How do we do that? Well, check out Philippians 2:3: "Do not let selfishness or pride be your guide. Be humble and give more honor to others than to yourselves" (ICB).

God wants us to think about other people, not just ourselves.

FiND It

IN THE BIBLE

LUKE 7:36–50

One day Jesus went to someone's house for dinner. Even though He was a guest, no one treated Him like one. Normally the host of the party would kiss the guest's cheek, put oil on his head, and make sure his feet were washed. But none of these things happened. Then a woman surprised Jesus by doing something very special to honor Him. She washed Jesus' feet, dried them with her hair, and kissed them. Then she got out a fancy jar of perfume that cost a lot of money and rubbed Jesus' feet with the perfume. She did more than anyone expected, just because she loved Jesus so much.

He wants us to care for other people's needs and feelings before our own.

Does that mean we are pushy, grumpy, or rude? No! Does that mean we complain about what people are doing or put them down? No!

Instead, we treat others with respect and use our manners. We listen to them and do things to help them—and do even more than what they expect from us. We might hold the door open for a long line of people or write a thank-you note to the school janitor. We want the people around us to feel special and loved because *they are*. God created them and loves them!

God, help me show respect and honor
for You and for other people.

TRY it OUT

The next time the kitchen table needs to be cleaned, start cleaning it without being asked. Then clean the kitchen floor too! You'll be honoring your family by doing it.

49

CHARACTER

noun   \ˈker-ik-tər\

who you
are inside

If a friend were to describe you, what would they say? Maybe they'd say you have long hair and wear glasses or your favorite thing to do is ride your bike or you're almost always laughing. All those things are ways to describe who you are.

But if someone wanted to know what your character is, they'd have to look closely at how you act—how you treat people, what kind of attitude you have, and whether you follow rules. Your character is who you are on the inside, and you show it by your choices.

What is God's character like? He's loving, patient, and kind. He's strong, wise, and fair. He's loyal, honest, and forgiving. How do we know that? He proves it by what He does.

God wants to help us change so that our character becomes like His character. He wants us to "see the difference between good and bad and choose the good" (Philippians 1:10 ICB). For example,

FiND It

IN THE BIBLE

1 SAMUEL 16

God told Samuel, "I've chosen one of Jesse's sons to be the new king. Go, and I'll show which one." Samuel saw eight sons. He thought God would point out a big and strong son, but instead God picked the youngest one, who didn't seem all that special. Why? Because "people look at the outside of a person, but the Lord looks at the heart" (1 Samuel 16:7 ICB). God could see what was in David's heart, and that's what mattered most.

if our friends want us to steal some candy with them, we'll know that's wrong, and we won't do it.

Having good character means doing the right thing even when it will make things harder for us, even when we're the only ones doing it, and even when no one but God can see us. Why? Because we're not doing good to make people like us. We're doing it because we care about what's right! We're strong, honest, and loving on the inside, so that's how we'll act in every situation.

God, make who I am on the inside—
my character—more like You.

TRY it OUT

Glue a few paperless crayons and a few regular lead pencils to the bottom of a cardboard box. Let the glue dry. Then, with a parent's help, use a hair dryer on the highest heat and blow hot air on them for several minutes. What happens? The crayons start to melt while the pencils stay the same. When we have good character, we're like the pencils. We can withstand the heat! We'll keep doing what's right even when it's hard.

PERSEVERANCE

noun   \ˌpər-sə-ˈvir-ən(t)s\

the power to keep going, even when it's hard

Have you ever run in a race? Everyone stands at a starting point. Someone yells, "Ready, set, go!" And *zoom*—everyone runs to the finish line!

Living a life of faith in God is like a race. The starting point is when we first believe, and the finish line is when we're in heaven. Between those two points, we show our faith by obeying God. But it's not a short race, and there will be times when we'll feel like giving up.

Sometimes people will make fun of us for obeying God, or we'll be the only ones doing what's right. But we don't have to let anyone push us into quitting—just like Jesus didn't. Were people ever mean to Him because He was obeying God? Yes. But did He ever give up? No!

Sometimes we'll be tempted to be selfish and just do whatever

FiND It
IN THE BIBLE

ACTS 14, 16, 27; 2 CORINTHIANS 11

Paul was often in danger as he traveled around telling people about Jesus. The people who didn't like his message would hurt him—they threw stones at him or put him in prison. Several times the ship Paul was in crashed. Even when things got hard, he kept obeying God. At the end of his life, Paul said, "I have fought the good fight. I have finished the race. I have kept the faith. Now, a crown is waiting for me" (2 Timothy 4:6–8 ICB).

we feel like. When that happens, what's our job? Perseverance! To never stop trying to follow God. To never give up on obeying Him. And don't worry—we don't have to do it alone! We can always pray and ask God to help us.

God allows problems and hard things in our lives because they are chances for us to grow. We get to practice trusting and obeying Him. Each time we do, we grow stronger and more patient.

So we keep running in the race because we're headed to an awesome finish line—heaven! Heaven will be so beautiful, with streets of gold and pearly gates, and God will give His people rewards, like crowns. But the best part? We'll be with God!

God, help me to have perseverance so that
I never give up on obeying You!

TRY it OUT

The next time you're doing a task you don't like doing, like brushing your teeth, think of it as a challenge. Do it because you know there will be a reward—no cavities! As you keep doing it every day, think of yourself being in a long race of doing what's right.

51

WILL

noun \wəl\

~~~

a plan or
desire for
what should
happen

All week you and your best friend make plans for Saturday. You're going to ride your bikes then play your favorite game while listening to loud music and eating popcorn and brownies. It's an awesome plan, and you can't wait!

God has a perfect plan for the world and everyone in it, and it's called His *will*. It's what He wants for His creation. He makes His plan happen, and sometimes He uses people to do it.

Jesus said that He came to earth to do what His Father wanted. He taught His disciples to pray for God's will to happen by saying, "Your kingdom come, your will be done, on earth as it is in heaven" (Matthew 6:10 NIV). That means, "Come do what You always do— what is right and best. We want whatever You want, God! Help us to do what is right too."

FiND It

IN THE BIBLE

MATTHEW 26

When it was time for Jesus to get ready to go to the cross, there was a part of Him that didn't want to do it. He knew it would be extremely painful. Then He said to God, "Yet not as I will, but as you will" (v. 39 NIV). That meant, "Do what you want, not what I want" (ICB). Jesus was saying yes to God's plan. He decided He would do whatever God said was best.

We learn about God's will in the Bible. God wants people to be able to say, "I'm free from sin because of Jesus!" He wants people to have happy hearts and say, "Thank You, God, for sunshine and strawberries and hugs!" He wants people to become superheroes of justice who say, "Let's make this fair." People who bring peace by saying, "I'll forgive you." And people who brighten up the world by saying, "I'll help" and "I love you."

God also has a perfect plan that is just for you. He wants to make the story of your life fit into His big story of the world. God says to you, "I will guide you along the best pathway for your life" (Psalm 32:8 NLT). He's got something wonderful in mind for you! And He'll be with you every step of the way.

God, thank You for Your perfect plans!

TRY it OUT

Draw a design on paper with a pencil. Then take crayons or markers, and color it, following the lines of your pencil drawing. Your pencil lines were the plan, like God's will. Your color marks followed the plan, just like when we obey and do what God wants.

52

GLORY

noun   \ˈglȯr-ē\

God's power,
beauty, and
perfection
on display

Have you ever sat still and just looked at the sky for a while? Maybe you saw puffy clouds moving quickly or a sunset with bright colors. The sky is so big and beautiful that it often makes us say, "Wow!"

Psalm 19:1 says, "The heavens tell the glory of God. And the skies announce what his hands have made" (ICB). They show how beautiful and powerful He is, don't they?

Whenever we see signs of what God is like, we're seeing His glory. We're getting a glimpse of what it's like to be with Him face to face. It makes us want to say, "Wow!"

We are part of God's creation—He made us—so we can "tell the glory of God" too. What does that mean exactly? It means we can help people see God's greatness. We won't do it the way a beautiful sky does, of course. Instead, we'll do it by the way we live.

When we obey God and live like Jesus, we show God's goodness.

FiND It

IN THE BIBLE

LUKE 2:8-14

After Jesus was born, an angel of the Lord visited shepherds. The Lord's glory shined all around them, and the shepherds became scared because it was so strange and powerful. But the angel said, "Don't be afraid. I have good news! It will bring joy to everybody. Your Savior has been born." Then a huge group of angels from heaven appeared too. They praised God, saying, "Give glory to God in heaven!" (v. 14 ICB).

When we're thankful for all He's done for us, we're pointing to His kindness. When we worship God in any way, it's like we're saying, "Look at how amazing He is! See how every good and wonderful thing comes from Him? He deserves the praise of the whole world. He's worth everyone's love and loyalty."

In heaven, we'll get to be with God face to face and see even more of His glory there. It will be so awesome that we'll keep wanting to say, "Wow! Wow! Wow!"

God, I want my life to show everyone Your glory so they can know how awesome You are.

TRY it OUT

Get a parent's help to find magazines with pictures of God's creation—the sky, seas, lakes, mountains, trees, forests, flowers, animals, and insects. Cut out your favorite pictures and glue them into a blank notebook. Just think: those are all special things God made. They're amazing! And the God who made them is even *more* amazing.

DEFINITIONS

BAPTISM: a special act using water that shows we've joined God's family

BIBLE: God's story and His message for us in writing

CHARACTER: who you are inside

CHURCH: all the people who believe in Jesus

COMMUNION: the acts of receiving and remembering Jesus by eating bread and drinking wine

CONFESS: to admit the wrong things we've done

COVENANT: an agreement of promises

CREATION: God's act of making something new

DISCIPLE: a student who learns from and becomes like their teacher

ETERNAL: having no beginning or end

FAITH: being sure about something you cannot see, touch, or hear

GLORY: God's power, beauty, and perfection on display

GOSPEL: the good news of salvation through Jesus

GRACE: something good that is not earned or expected

HEAVEN: God's home and kingdom

HOLY: pure and set apart

HONOR: showing someone they're important

HOPE: looking forward to good things in the future

IDOL: anything or anyone we treat as more important than God

JOY: a gladness about God and His goodness

JUSTICE: what is right and fair for everyone

LAW: the rules God gave Israel to make the Israelites righteous and loving

LOVE: wanting goodness for someone and working to bring it to them

MERCY: a choice to not give the punishment someone deserves

MIRACLE: something God does to show His power

OBEDIENCE: the act of doing what God says to do

PARABLE: a story that teaches a truth about God

PEACE: a state of living without fear or fighting

PERSEVERANCE: the power to keep going, even when it's hard

PHARISEE: a Jewish leader focused on following rules

PRAYER: a talk with God

PRIDE: the thought that you're better than you are or more important than others

PROPHECY: a message from God spoken by a person

PSALM: a song or poem that is a prayer to God

RECONCILIATION: the act of bringing together two people whose friendship is broken

REDEMPTION: the act of buying back

RESURRECTION: coming back to life after dying

RIGHTEOUSNESS: being perfect and always right

SABBATH: God's special day of rest

SACRIFICE: something given up and offered as a gift

SALVATION: a rescue from sin and a new life with God

SANCTIFICATION: the process of becoming holier

SIN: an action that God says is wrong

SOVEREIGNTY: God's power and right to rule everything

TABERNACLE: a beautiful tent for God to live in

TEMPTATION: a feeling of being pulled toward doing something bad

TRINITY: God the Father, God the Son, and God the Holy Spirit

WILL: a plan or desire for what should happen

WISDOM: the ability to know and do what God says is right

WITNESS: someone who sees or hears about something and then tells others about it

WORKS: the good things we do that please God

WORSHIP: giving praise and showing honor